KEEP GOING!

A Collection of Inspirational Stories and Practical Advice For Women to Persevere Powerfully through Challenges & Create Magic Out Of Any Mess!

UNIVERSAL IMPACT PRESS

KEEP GOING!

A Collection of Inspirational Stories and Practical Advice For Women to Persevere Powerfully through Challenges & Create Magic Out Of Any Mess!

Visionary Author:

Aisha Wonderfull

Contributing Authors:

A. Felicity Darville
Alicia Hernandez
C.R. Lundy
Denise D. Beneby
Ednica Newbold
Kay Charlton Cleare
Krista Barr-Bastian
Olivia Munroe Ferguson
Tashoy Walters
Virginia Somerville

Copyright © 2022 Technicolor Blossom LLC

All Rights Reserved.

No part of this book may be reproduced in any form or by any means without prior written permission from the publisher.

Published by: Universal Impact Press

www.UniversalImpactPress.com

DEDICATION

This book is dedicated to all women who have their eyes set on a brighter future, even though they may be currently in darkness.

May you always seek the Lord to order your steps, and as you travel the path that He has set out before you, no matter the challenges that arise, may you always *KEEP GOING*.

Contents

INTRODUCTION
Aisha Wonderfull — 10

MENTAL & EMOTIONAL WELL BEING — 16

Ruach – "Breathe"
Author: Ednica Newbold — 17

Broken But Mended
Author: Kay Charlton Cleare — 31

MONEY, WEALTH & ABUNDANCE — 52

Making Money Appear Out of Thin Air
Author: A. Felicity Darville — 53

RELATIONSHIPS — 64

You Are Not Alone
Author: Virginia Somerville — 65

RESILIENCE & PERSEVERANCE — 80

Push Purposefully!
Author: Krista Barr-Bastian — 81

When Strength Was All I Knew
Author: Olivia Munroe Ferguson — 93

Your Faith Has Healed You
Author: Tashoy Walters — 107

Contents

SPIRITUALITY — 119

God's Peace
Author: Alicia Hernandez — 120

Churched Out
Author: C.R. Lundy — 134

Unwavering Faith
Author: Denise D. Beneby — 148

SUMMARY — 165

ABOUT THE AUTHORS — 168

Aisha "Wonderfull" — 169

A. Felicity Darville — 172

Alicia Hernandez — 175

C.R. Lundy — 177

Denise D. Beneby — 179

Ednica Newbold — 182

Kay Charlton Cleare — 185

Contents

ABOUT THE AUTHORS (continued)

Krista Barr-Bastian	187
Olivia Munroe Ferguson	189
Tashoy Walters	192
Virginia Somerville	195

Introduction

KEEP GOING!

INTRODUCTION

Aisha Wonderfull

It was a hot summer day in Nassau Bahamas. I was a young girl, just 11 years old. I had recently graduated from elementary school and was now in high school! However, the joy I felt in officially being a little more grown-up was very quickly evaporating in the summer heat.

We were in physical education class, and to my surprise, the assignment for the class was to complete a cross-country run across the school's immense campus. "Are you kidding me??" was all I could think at the time. Even the excitement from bonding immediately with a brand-new friend in this new environment couldn't dampen my annoyance. I was not a runner. I was not athletic. Plus, we just got here! We didn't even know the campus that well. What if we got lost?? And we were just little kids! But they wanted us to run around this whole entire campus?

KEEP GOING!

From what I could tell, everyone else seemed to have the same reaction, well at least most of the girls. The boys seemed to shrug off the task and they soon sped off as the rest of us girls started to shuffle reluctantly along.

But then my new friend startled me as she picked up an easy stride. "Oh goodness!" I groaned to myself inside. She actually looked like she wanted to run this cross-country as best she could! Not wanting to show my true feelings, I reluctantly kept up with her pace, even though it was much harder for me than it seemed to be for her. Several minutes in, we had already passed most of the girls and had caught up with some of the boys. I was surprised at myself. Never in a million years would I have ever thought I could have run as much as I had run in just those few short minutes.

A few more minutes passed and this time I was starting to struggle, for real. I was able to gasp out to her: "Let's stop and walk for a bit." I was proud of myself at that point – I had kept up the best I was able to, and we were well on our way. But I was truly tired. I couldn't go on running any longer. My lungs were on fire, my legs were aching and I couldn't keep

KEEP GOING!

up the pace. But to my horror – she said – Let's keep going for a little bit more.

So I pushed myself, and we kept going for a little more, before stopping to walk for a few minutes.

That continued for the rest of the way. We would run at her pace, I would go until the point I could not go on any further, and then she would still push us to keep going. And somehow, I was able to do just that. I was able to keep going.

In about 20 minutes, we were all done. The reward was to enjoy the rest of the class time to just relax and hang out, as the others slowly made their way in. And boy did we enjoy it!! It was a different experience for me. It was the first time I could ever remember having a friend encourage me to do more than I thought I was able to. It was the first time someone else other than my parents encouraged me to keep going.

In all the wisdom of an 11-year-old, I knew that what I had experienced was something special. Something timeless. As I gazed over at my new friend, I felt joy and

KEEP GOING!

gratitude for having her in my life. Today, 33 years later, I still have the same joy and gratitude that I did that warm August day in 1989; that new friend I made turned out to become my very best friend. And just as she did then, she has continued to push and encourage me to keep going…..especially during the times when I think I can't go on any longer.

Sharing Our Stories

I can confidently say to you, that if you have come across this book, it is by no accident. Maybe you are struggling with a challenging time in life, and have come to the end of your rope. Maybe this book has come across your path at this particular time so that the examples of other women and the advice and wisdom they share with you can strengthen and encourage you to Keep Going. In this book, which is categorized by themes, you will undoubtedly find the specific story that speaks directly to you. In their own styles, in their own voices, and from their own unique perspectives, each of the contributing authors shares powerful lessons

KEEP GOING!

learned from their own challenges, as an inspiring message for you.

As a native of The Bahamas, this book is truly an example of the Bahamian motto to move Forward, Upward, Onward....*TOGETHER*. Through this book, I have linked arms and held hands with these 10 amazing co-authors as we have done just that.... by stepping forward *together* to share our stories with you.

I know that as you read through this book, the stories and examples of these amazing and powerful women will touch a chord deep inside of you. And undoubtedly, you will remember your own strength, your own power that has been instilled and passed down to you.

It is my hope that this remembrance will propel you to step powerfully into your own unique place, and in your own way as a mentor, guide in your own right, and take up the mantle of showing up for others in a special way that is unique to you.

Are you ready?! It's time!

KEEP GOING!

It is time to step forward, time to move upward and onward, *together* as we share with you the stories of how to **Keep Going.**

Our Stories

KEEP GOING!

Mental & Emotional Well-Being

KEEP
GOING!

KEEP GOING!

Ruach "Breathe"

Author: Ednica Newbold

"Prophesy over these bones, and say to them, O dry bones, hear the word of the Lord. Thus says the Lord God to these bones: Behold, I will cause breath to enter you, and you shall live. - Ezekiel 37:4-5"

Life can be so chaotic that sometimes, we forget to "Breathe". Most of us are so wrapped up in the routine of striving and surviving that we retreat and resume our days without taking intentional breaths. Whatever is going on right now, take a moment to escape from your reality and in 5,6,7,8 - Breathe!

The intentional breath you just took is a life-giving gift that most of us take for granted. Breathing infuses oxygen into your lungs, flows through your veins, pulsates your heart, and permeates your soul while also collecting waste to expel as you exhale! Breathing is essential to life. No matter what your circumstances are know that you are still victorious because YOU ARE HERE! You proved it just now by BREATHING!

KEEP GOING!

Life in itself is a gift. One that most of us take for granted. I know it sounds cliche as most sayings do, but we never truly appreciate the value of something until we lose it. But as precious as life is, it throws many blows our way.

The tumultuous storms of life rage a seemingly never-ending war that sometimes causes you to want to surrender your flag in defeat or perhaps be thrown into the depths of the sea like Jonah. What do you do when life knocks the wind out of you? How do you keep pressing forward when everything around you is shattering and you feel broken beyond recognition and repair? How can you hold on to faith when life travesties reveal that you have none left to cling to?

These are some heavy questions and I'm sure most of us have stood at this crossroads at some point in our lives. So, what exactly causes some people to drown in their sorrows and others to swim ashore? I don't have an exact response because everyone's situation is different. We all process and move through devastation differently. But one thing we do have in common is breath - "Ruach"!

KEEP GOING!

Ruach ("roo-akh") is the Hebrew word for God's breath. It also means to blow, to breathe, to perceive, and has also been used to refer to wind or spirit. As I reflect on my own experiences of no longer wanting to exist because of the perils of life, Ruach is the most astounding theme to my triumph because that is exactly what God did; He breathed life into my situation and miraculously transformed my mourning into dancing.

It is my hope that as I share my own story of emptiness and despair I breathe life, hope, release, restoration, and miracles into your soul.

K.O - Knocked Out

"Oops! I didn't see that coming!" 2021 came to ANNIHILATE me! I started the year with a bang! Excited to accomplish everything I undoubtedly knew God placed within me. This was going to be my most ambitious and accomplished year yet! I was prepared to trust the process, get out of my way and move in obedience even when I didn't see a way or know the "how". My theme for 2021 was QUANTUM LEAP! It was the year I would completely

KEEP GOING!

surrender, walk out my faith and catapult into purpose! Well, so I thought! I even formally registered my passion project, "Cultivate Your Garden" as a business in January, as I was determined that it was time to till the ground, plant seeds and yield an abundant harvest.

But instead of blazing a trail into the year, by the end of March, I was depleted, dejected, and DEPRESSED! How?!?! How could this be? And why me? I wish I could give you a specific answer but many micro-storms, which I thought I had plowed through, amalgamated into a tsunami that wiped me out! My marriage was on the rocks, I was questioning my identity and life choices and paralyzed with fear of moving in any direction.

On the surface, I appeared to be weathering the storm well, ducking and dodging any blows that came my way. I tried my best to save face with those around me. Covid made this pretty easy to achieve with isolating. Even though the sleepless nights, increased anxiety, delusional thinking, and panic attacks were all indications that I was sinking, I continued to set sail convinced that I would eventually get

KEEP GOING!

through this transition season. The signs were blatantly present but I kept going without taking a moment to pause, reflect, breathe, and reassess. After two months of getting pounded in the ring of life, it became more evident that I was losing this match as I became unfunctional in my daily affairs. I had no choice but to stop everything - working, socializing and parenting. Sadly, this was also my K.O. moment. There was nothing left for me to give and certainly no reason to live. Life knocked the wind out of me, leaving me breathless.

Catch Your Breath

I wish I could tell you that things got better, that this was the moment I got in the corner mustered all of my strength, dusted off my faith, and struck life back breaking through my despair. Instead, it got real dark and gloomy before even a sliver of light appeared. I had no desire to live and no faith to stand on. Zero faith! I was anti-religious, anti-Christianity, and anti-God. Although I believed in God, I was convinced that I was worthless and God's wrath was upon me. These thoughts and feelings made me feel worst because I knew better! I was a Christian, so how did I end up here? How

KEEP GOING!

could this be me? The girl with such a zeal for life and faith in God. The one who grew up in church - children's choir, youth choir, bible study, Sunday school, and Friday night youth groups - I was there. But here I was discouraged, deeply depressed, and FAITHLESS! The last thing I wanted to hear about was God or anything biblical. I couldn't even stomach listening to gospel music. I lost my luster for life. From my perspective, all hope was gone. Eventually, I became obsessed with a desire to terminate my life as I believed and felt that was the only way of escape.

I needed the break. There was no way I could have continued without it as it was hard for me to focus and perform throughout the day and I was operating on little sleep. I got maybe 2 hours of sleep (if that) at night. Instead of using the pause to catch my breath, shift my environment and open up in therapy, I isolated myself which allowed my thoughts to consume me. I also manipulated my way through therapy by telling my therapists half-truths and hiding how deep in the pit I was. I tried multiple therapists to no avail because I was not honest. I was afraid of what might occur if I opened up

KEEP GOING!

because my thoughts were not logical and somewhat delusional. Yet they were real to me.

Sometimes in life, we have to throw in the towel or at least modify our schedules, so that we can take care of ourselves. You are not required to be strong all the time or carry this burden alone as this too can lead to burnout and feelings of despair and hopelessness. But you also shouldn't isolate yourself to the point that there is no entryway for light to shine in the midst of your darkness. It is necessary that we take time to catch our breath, especially when the load seems too heavy to bear.

Catching your breath gives you the opportunity to rest, reassess, recuperate, and pivot if needed. It helps you to clear through the fog and brings clarity to your situation. By catching your breath you are creating a space to challenge those thoughts and gather the strength needed to proceed. Some ways in which we can catch our breath include:

- Confiding in someone trustworthy,
- Asking for assistance when needed,
- Being open to therapy or counseling,

KEEP GOING!

- Getting away for some rest and relaxation,
- Breathing exercises and meditation,
- Spending time in nature or
- Doing an activity you enjoy.

When life boxes you around, destabilizes, and disorients you, perhaps it is an indication that you should retreat to your corner of the ring, before attempting to deliver the next blow. Even the most skilled fighter knows how to return to their corner, catch their breath and enable their corner man to refuel, reenergize and reignite their desire to fight back! You don't have to go at it alone! There is always a corner providing an escape even if just for a moment and there is always a cornerman. Your cornerman can be someone you trust, God, or both. When choosing a person as your cornerman make sure that person is trustworthy, dependable, and available. By available, I mean they have the capacity to help you offload because some people although willing to be there for you, may be burdened with their own struggles, thereby unable to provide the support you need. You want to be able to release the load without judgment or recourse.

KEEP GOING!

Your cornerman wears many hats. He is your coach, hype man, nurse, and strategist. He is your coach guiding you through the emotional rollercoaster of preparing for battle. As your hype man, he is devoted to seeing you win and knows exactly what to say to motivate you and ignite your victorious mindset. As your medic or nurse, your cornerman tends to your wounds and aids in your recovery with the goal of maximizing your oxygen intake through the use of controlled breathing techniques.

He is your strategist, observing your actions and the movements of your opponent, and providing tactical advice necessary to win the match. The corner man though sitting on the sidelines is so instrumental to the outcome of the fight that the best corner man you can bring to any match is God. He is omnipresent, the great physician, all-knowing, and the ultimate undefeated champion.

Little Faith - No Faith

You now know how imperative it is to catch your breath before moving ahead, as it can propel you to victory or contribute to your faltering defeat. But what if you are so deep

KEEP GOING!

in despair that you simply cannot catch your breath? You have little to no faith at all that the mere thought of even attempting to do seems impossible. Does this mean that you will falter to your defeat?

Most of us are familiar with the scripture pertaining to mustard seed faith. *"If you have faith as small as a mustard seed, you can say to this mountain, 'Move from here to there,' and it will move. Nothing will be impossible for you."* *(Matthew 17:20)* It is used to encourage people to hold on even if they are hanging by a thread. It may look like you are defeated and surrounded by your troubles. It seems like everything that could go wrong went wrong. But if I can just cling to my faith, no matter how small, then that flicker of hope would invoke a positive change.

Sometimes it seems impossible to muster up even a tiny speck of a mustard seed. You may find yourself tumbling deeper and deeper into the pit. You might even pitch a tent there because from your perspective all hope is gone. This was my lot at the height of my depression. The only relief for me was to escape life itself. It would be better for everyone

KEEP GOING!

including me if I were no longer here. I was so lost in the abyss that a mustard seed faith was nowhere in sight, even though God kept throwing me lifelines my mind was too cluttered to perceive and receive them. Thankfully that didn't stop Him from reaching in and pulling me out of the pit.

Focusing solely on the mustard seed faith is dangerous when you are mentally distressed because its focal point is YOUR faith. This can render you worthless and doomed because you have no faith when in reality it doesn't have to be your faith. I know personally if it were up to my faith I would not be here and if I was, I certainly wouldn't be coherent. When night's overwhelming darkness is hovering over you remember you don't have to sit in the dark alone. The paralyzed man was healed because of the faith of his friends. It was not his faith that save him but those around him.

Even if you happened to isolate yourself so much that those around you can no longer be found there is still hope. Jesus also healed the man's son in order to invoke his faith. *"I do believe, help me overcome my unbelief!"* (Mark 9:24) This statement by the boy's father resonates so much with me

KEEP GOING!

because in hindsight that is exactly how I felt. I believed in God, but I also believed in the negative thoughts I had. My belief in God went as far as knowing He existed, but I did not concern myself with any of His attributes. The impending doom was so prevalent and I was certain there was no way out.

The Healing Power in God's Breath

Ruach is most commonly used to describe God's breath or His Spirit. Each of us has His breath within us. Genesis 1:7 says, *"And the LORD God formed man of the dust of the ground, and breathed into his nostrils the breath of life; and man became a living soul"*. Not only did God create us in His image and likeness; but it is His breath that sustains our souls. His spirit is within us and His presence surrounds us. By drawing on this power we can indeed bring life to those dry bones, whatever your bones may be: health issues, marital woes, financial difficulties, or mental illness.

In our weakness, He is strong. We need God's breath when our own strength fails us. He finishes where we left off. Ruach catches us up to who we originally are, our divine

KEEP GOING!

being. These intentional breaths can ground us and help us remember that our spiritual being is perfect and all is well. Regardless of what is going on we can steady ourselves and find assurance in knowing that ALL THINGS work out for good.

As we breathe in, we allow the purification process to occur both spiritually and physically. When you INHALE imagine God's Spirit as a ray of light entering your lungs and flowing through your veins releasing grace wherever it is needed. Hold for a few seconds and while holding visualize that light uncovering some hidden patches and is working away at repairing the holes, depositing grace according to the measure needed.

During the repair process, toxins contributing to the patches are gathered for expulsion. When you exhale, imagine that these toxins (negative thinking, anxiety, depression) are being released from your body. Everything that was eating away at you and weighing you down was released when you exhale. You begin to feel lighter and you feel the load lifting and the atmosphere shifting. You are LIGHT! There's a

KEEP GOING!

heavenly glow around you because not only have you found the light but you BECOME the light all because you took the time to catch your breath and remember your superpower - RUACH!

KEEP GOING!

"Broken But Mended"

Author: Kay Charlton Cleare

Hurt is defined as a cause of injury or damage. It is also known to be inflicted with physical pain or suffering. It strikes you unexpectedly and leaves you with the taste of defeat. It has the intent to kill, steal and destroy. Hurt can cause mental distress and anguish.

Its potential has erupted and hardened so many hearts across the globe. Understand this one fact, people don't realize that feelings are temporary so they hold onto them and allow them to become permanent. It is in that very moment of experiencing your level of hurt that can totally take over your mind without thinking. Its effect can put you in a place so deep, so dark, so lonely, so sad, so empty. Some situations can make you or break you but you must always know that you

KEEP GOING!

are in control of your life. And in knowing you must keep running towards the purpose behind your pain.

In our life, we women experience hurt in so many ways. In relationships, families, losing a loved one, being betrayed…. there are so many ways I can go on with. You see, hurt is an emotional study caused by words or actions. We have totally missed the way to keep going instead of keeping blaming. It's time for us to rise above our feelings and see life in the fragile state that it meets us, let us avoid blaming others for how we take things and start expressing how the situation made us feel. This is the way forward to avoiding hurt and in avoiding or fixing HURT we then avoid HATE. It is indeed a fact that so many people have been affected by hurt and over time the hurt developed into hate.

My Story

As a girl growing up, I had to follow the house rules. One was to be up and ready for church. Sitting attentively listening to the preacher (my grandfather, the late Rev. Edwin Charlton) I remember a passage, taken from the book of Matthew 18:6: *But whoso shall offend one of these little ones*

KEEP GOING!

which believe in me, it were better for him that a millstone was hanged about his neck, and that he was drowned in the depth of the sea. The reason why I shared this particular scripture will become clear very soon.

From a very tender age, I suffered in silence. As a young girl, I had dreams of growing up to be a great woman, wife, mother, and contributor in my country. With very little knowledge of what the world had to offer, I often used my imagination to create a world in my head. In this imaginary world of mine, I was a strong woman who was an inspiration to others, a wife of a King, a mother of 3 beautiful children, a lawyer, and a business owner. There I was residing in one of the 700 islands of the Bahamas with hopes and aspirations of a fairy tale ending someday.

But to my surprise, I would soon have to reevaluate my dreams. I was about 9 years old when my father decided to leave my mom, brother, and me, behind to move to the Capital city for a better opportunity. This was a very hard pill for me to swallow but I did. Every night I cried myself asleep hoping that when I woke my father would be back (but that

KEEP GOING!

little girl's tears kept flowing until she decided that he was not coming back for her). The word was out on the small island that I lived on that my dad had moved away. But what I didn't know was that I was about to find out who were the perverts on the land as I soon become their prey, without a father to defend me.

The island predators made themselves known to me. With fear in my eyes, I was now faced with some of the neighbors and a few family members touching and crawling over my skin like serpents. I was now a victim of molestation. Vulnerable without a voice I cried in silence. I yearned to scream for help but how could I when my offender told me they will kill me and my family, I was just a child in fear of losing anyone else I love.

With my mother now being the breadwinner for my brother and me, I felt like my problem would become another problem for her and the family, so I didn't tell her what was going on. I couldn't risk my family being killed, as my offender told me. You see my mother was a nonsense woman,

KEEP GOING!

she would tear my hip up just because; for her, giving me a beating was her solution even when a solution wasn't needed.

So many times, I would hide away or pretend to be busy when I was called upon to go to certain families to take goods from the farm or to the store because of the fear of serpents crawling over my skin and sometimes leaving fluids on my body. I didn't understand what was happening but I knew it was something bad. This went on for a few years until my great-grandmother got sick and my mother had to move into the capital city of Nassau to be her caretaker. Finally! I said to myself, I can be a normal child again. But this would only last for a short time before I discovered that serpents also lived in the city of Nassau. With fear and disappointment, I sobbed knowing that I had moved away from my nightmare only to become prey to another family molester and rapist.

As a young girl, there I was again standing in the lane of prey needing prayers in my place of brokenness, fear, and distress. I gathered the courage to stand up to my abuser, and told him I am going to the police, to which he replied, I will burn the house down and shoot up everyone while you're

KEEP GOING!

asleep. I was so distressed and despondent at my unsuccessful attempt to scare my abuser away, all I could do was cry out to the Lord: "Why Me???" I was a good child, always helpful and kind, I could not understand why God allowed these things to keep happening to me?

At this point in my life, I became bitter, I barely spoke and I became very defensive and I didn't trust anyone. I had developed resentment as thoughts of bitterness and negativity ran through my mind, and I wondered why someone in my family couldn't recognize what was happening to me.

I thought I had already faced the worst until one weekend I was allowed to go with my family members to an event. It was around 9:30 pm and my aunties wanted to stay out so they decided to let me take a ride home with a male friend of the family. I was furious and wanted to stay because the only thing that crossed my mind was "Will I be prey to another serpent?"

While in his car I felt like we had been driving for hours, then he pulled up by a beach that seemed like it was in the back of nowhere, he held a knife to my throat and told me

KEEP GOING!

not to make a sound. As he crawled on top of me and devoured my innocence, I felt numb and I remembered the tears rolling down my face. My spirit cried Lord how much more? The next thing I remembered was being dropped off at home, where my uncle was waiting out front. He asked the male family friend where my aunties were, and he replied still out.

I then had a 2nd predator for that night as my uncle took me behind a warehouse building next door and crawled upon me, servings himself of my innocence. I screamed but no one came to my rescue, I cried but no one heard, at this time I was mentally, physically, and emotionally dead.

I asked myself how could a 15-year-old be double raped in the same night and have no one to fight her battles? Fear overtook me as he told me never to say a word, and I did not want anyone getting hurt because of me talking; I was also fearful of being the cause of destruction, and also thought that maybe no one will ever believe me. I suffered in silence; I had a constant, unbearable, uncomfortable, unwanted, hurt, and fearful, feeling all the time. The feeling of low self-esteem and brokenness. I desired to go to a time when I could feel whole

KEEP GOING!

again, live again, dream again, and get the opportunity to grow up like other young girls, but I would soon realize that the time has passed for that.

The day finally came when I was able to go and live with my aunty, and my soul rejoiced! My new living situation was far from perfect, but I felt like I could finally breathe again. I no longer had to face my fears every day, and I no longer had to live in the same space as my pervert.

My Experience

All my life I learned that men were created to be great, to love, to provide, and protect. But in my early childhood, some of them left bitterness within me because they didn't protect me, but instead hurt me and took my innocence from me. As a young girl that was brought up in a Godly environment, I would often question why the men around me were not living as I read in the Bible.

I saw men as poor, disappointing, unsatisfactory, and ordinary when I should have seen them as the head and strong leaders that God placed them among us to be. The only man I

KEEP GOING!

saw in the image of God was my grandfather. And he was the inspiration and the hope that I grasped onto, with the hopes that all of the other men that are not child molesters, and are more like him.

As I bloomed into my teenage years, I realized that I became defensive and suspicious, and my communication was on time out. No one understood me, because the girl within me was at war with who she is. I was a lost child bogged down in fear, pain, and shame that I didn't ask for.

Many times, I would try different things and avenues trying to put the broken pieces of my life back together but I would always run into a dead end. Life was not easy for me because I wasn't able to relate and connect with others effectively, not because I couldn't, but because of fear, having my feeling hurt, or because I felt like no one would understand or believe me.

Having conversations with people was always uncomfortable, to get me to talk and casually converse with someone was like pulling a tooth with me. At that time in my life, I had developed the 4 levels of temperament, and with 4

KEEP GOING!

different personalities, it was impossible to keep up with or understand me. Even today I find myself when facing a hurtful situation wanting to shut down and close the accessibility and communication off but I don't because I now know how to overcome the fear of hurt and find healing from it.

I would always feel dirty, ashamed, unworthy, useless, inadequate, insecure, and even embarrassed to accept my past. I was so insecure about my body because for me it reflected my hurt. Uncertainty met me in every situation of life because I never trusted anyone.

My Path to Freedom: Forgiveness

It took me almost 18 years to find myself, to discover who I am, and to be set free from a broken childhood. It started with me telling myself I didn't deserve what I had to go through, and knowing that the time had come for me to let go of the years of resentment and fear that had me confined, restrained, bound, and trapped.

As an adult, I was at the place of confession acknowledging that I allowed the molestations that happened

KEEP GOING!

to me to go on for so long because I was afraid of the faces and words of men. I realized that my life was being held up by the years of trauma and emotions I secretly and shamefully endured, but I vowed to release the pain, fear and hurt that I carried for all the years and I FORGAVE my molesters.

Forgiving them has given me a life beyond my physical eyes and now I know what freedom feels and looks like. I can truly say that forgiveness is the key to the best you ever. Forgiving someone who has caused you a tremendous amount of physical, mental, emotional and spiritual pain and damage is not easy, it's one of the most difficult steps to take but it is also one of the best decisions and things you can step into and display in your life. Before I came to the place of forgiveness, I was a walking dead because I was so heavy with the weight of destruction and hate. Forgiveness was my path to freedom, my path to being able to experience life in the full beauty of all that it had for me.

I've learned that most predators are family or close friends. Unfortunately, the hurt usually comes from those you cherish and look to for protection. I was the little girl suffering

KEEP GOING!

without a way out, left feeling inadequate and uncertain about everything and everyone that I came in contact with because of my experiences.

I wanted revenge but I never got it. I was often frustrated and angry. For so long I wanted my pain to end but did not know how to, but I've learned that everything is a process. And that nothing is guaranteed to last forever so I found my fix in forgiving, accepting what I went through, getting past my worst nightmare of fear, and understanding that I was the one who was standing in the way of my own healing.

Through my experience, I've learned to keep going and to fight to become the woman I used to dream about becoming as a child. I've learned to keep going even if I can't see my way out. Wanting to stop and give up may often cross our minds but giving up will never hold a place in my space and I will keep going no matter the pain or the cost because I know there's something greater for me in pushing through my brokenness to my season of healing.

KEEP GOING!

Today, I no longer stand in a fearful place but I stand in a place of experience where I now have a voice to speak up and speak out, and I am here to stand up for you.

For I know what Luke 1:37 says' *'For nothing is impossible with God,* and I know what Romans 12:19 say' *Do not take revenge, my dear friends, but leave room for God's wrath, for it is written:'It is mine to avenge; I will repay"* says the Lord.

My Lesson for You

No matter how bad the situation seems or gets, you have to find a way to tell someone about it. Hidden pain and trauma can mentally and physically leave some unwanted scars on your life. Trauma will have you second-guessing who you are, your value, and your future. It can easily overtake your mind and your emotional well-been.

During my healing process, I've had to accept myself as a whole and had to let go of every emotion and thought that was stagnating my healing process. Never blame yourself for a situation you did not create but be careful of wearing the

KEEP GOING!

blame as though it's a part of you. Life has so many tests that we have to face but sometimes we see them from a different light and we dare not to accept the fact that all they are is transportation to our appointed destination.

I am a survivor of child abuse. Yes, I thought about suicide. Yes, anxiety had me confined. Yes, I had mood changes. Yes, I had low self-esteem. But did it kill me? No. Did I overcome it? Yes. Was it easy? No. Did I give up? No, I kept going.

You see every women's strength is different, and we all deal with trauma differently but one thing remains, when we cannot stand up for ourselves we need someone to stand for us. When it hurts so much and we cannot find the words for ourselves to give us the comfort and surety that we won't have to go through it again, that we won't have to hurt much longer. But how do we get surety of a better tomorrow without surety of a safe today?

Mothers, we have to find our active place in the life of our children, especially daughters, it's very necessary and needed. Mothers, we are the strength for our daughters, we are

KEEP GOING!

the force that drives them into knowing their worth and understanding how to face fears as they come and not allow it to linger within them. We have to be the eyes our daughter needs, we have to become the watchmen over our children's physical and mental future, spiritually, mentally, and physically.

No, we cannot be with them every minute but we can make them feel like we are their safe place. Let us love our children unconditionally so that no matter what they share with us we will be able to still love and see them in the way a mother should, support them through their most difficult times and situations, and always believe what your child tells you about abuse.

By God's grace, I finally came to a place where I had to admit to myself that I have overcome what happened to me but I also know that I will never forget. I learned to not allow myself to lose out on life opportunities because of anger. I chose to get up, get dressed, put on my armors, and keep going, and if I was able to do it, I want you to know that you can too.

KEEP GOING!

I Am Here For You

To every girl and woman that was molested or raped, I want you to know that:

1. Am sorry this happened to you.

2. You are not responsible for what happened to you.

3. I believe you.

4. What happened to you does not define who you are, you are still just as valuable and beautiful as before.

5. Take my hands, I'll walk with you through this because I know the feeling oh too well.

6. I know it's not easy, in fact, the thought of it is unforgettable and frightening.

7. You are strong enough to get past and overcome your trauma.

8. Never allow your situation to permanently affect you. You *must* keep going.

KEEP GOING!

9. You are here for a bigger purpose, trust the process and take on every situation with the intent to overcome.

10. As your bright future awaits your arrival know that your past pain has no place in your present and it lost its value from the season of its time.

Finding the Purpose in Your Pain

Ladies, as hard as it is to accept, we cannot control what or how things happen to us but we can be the voice for those voices that cries without a sound, for those that are too afraid to find their healing, for those that yearn for someone to understand them even when they don't understand themselves. Let us stand together today for a better tomorrow for ourselves and our daughters. And no matter what we must keep going.

To every woman that mothers a child/children, I know that mothering is not easy, it can get so unbearable and overwhelming to the point where it makes you feel like giving up, but I encourage you to keep going as I did. I understand the challenges that life dishes out to use and the long road that

KEEP GOING!

we travel to get to our desired destination, may make us weary and tired, but believe me when I tell you that it's all a part of a bigger purpose.

Many tears will drop from your eyes when you have to balance children, home, church, work, school, business, and life challenges. I am a mother of 1 son and 2 daughters and I know firsthand how overwhelming it can be trying to juggle their own demands while still maintaining your other daily duties. But please believe me mothers - when GOD gives our kind the power to conceive and bear children, He gifts us with the ability to nurture, withstand, and love unselfishly. My plea is for you to take an extra minute today, no matter how much you have on your plate to hear your children, to spend some extra time to see your children and to learn and understand your children no matter how your day was.

Mothers, sometimes you have to ask hard questions if you notice a change in your children's behavior and do whatever it takes to find a way to hear their inner cry. Yes, I know that you have been making sacrifices for so many years for a better tomorrow for your children but what good is

KEEP GOING!

tomorrow if they can't mentally get past today? Our daughters are hurting (even some of our sons). Some of them are hurting victims looking for a way out, waiting for a freedom call, and wishing it was ok to trust someone enough.

Mothers, many of us are victims of our past traumas. Some of you may have faced similar situations that I did, maybe you kept going to reach a place of freedom as I did or maybe you are still broken and don't know how to put the pieces together and heal for your generation. But let me just tell you right now that you are strong enough to conquer and overpower the devil's destruction and strongholds from over your life and your generations.

Feeling destroyed from the inside always shows on the outside. Mothers, it's past time that we diligently seek God and ask Him not just for the strength to move forward but the ability to relate effectively in order to bring healing not just to ourselves but to those that we are appointed to.

So many times, as women and young girls you yearned for someone to recognize your pain because you are too broken to find your voice. It is you that I am here to reach, it

KEEP GOING!

is you that I had to keep going for, and understand that my experience was about me overcoming my pain and trauma so that I could be here today, standing into my own freedom, to be able to encourage, motivate, and guide you to your own deliverance and freedom.

Yes! This message is for YOU! It is time! This is your season to begin your own journey to freedom, to forgive, to overcome fear, and to keep going no matter what, as I did.

Mothers let us learn to always be on guard for the innocence of our children. In today's reality, we have to now protect our daughters and our from the hands of predators. For truly what was in the beginning so shall it be in the end. You see for so many decades families have swept molestation and rape under the rug and expected the victims to live with the shame and carry the guilt that they did not choose. Today I stand fully armed to fight the hidden secrets of so many girls, boys, and women across the globe.

To all the women and girls who have been abused, maybe your experience has left you mentally disturbed, physically broken, and spiritually weak. It's not your fault to

KEEP GOING!

feel the way you do. But I need you to reach deep within and reconnect with the person that God has created and placed you in this world to be. Accept the fact that you have no control over other people's decisions. Admit what happened to you, and I want you to know that it's not the end of your life it's the beginning of someone else freedom. Face your fear knowing that it no longer holds you in captivity. And find your healing through forgiveness.

I encourage you to stop accepting being a victim and walk with confidence into your healing season with the confidence to overcome and find your smile again. I overcame what happened to me and kept going so that I can be strength and an anchor of hope for some young girl or woman that finds these words. My prayer is for you too to *KEEP GOING*, so that you too can pass on the baton to another.

KEEP GOING!

Money, Wealth & Abundance

KEEP GOING!

KEEP GOING!

"Making Money Appear Out of Thin Air"

Author: Felicity Darville

There's something special about Autumn leaves. The colors are fascinating. They create a breathtaking landscape. They are light and playful and fly freely about in the wind. They can evoke emotion and lead to inspiration. I love Autumn leaves. But, I live in The Bahamas, so I don't get to see the beautiful colors that signal the fall. However, you can tell when it's Autumn here. We get more breeze - a relief from the hot summer season.

It was in a flurry of Autumn leaves one breezy afternoon that I manifested money out of thin air. Sounds impossible? Well, nothing is too great for God.

At the time, I was a divorced mother of four. I worked for myself, and so every day I had to push and make sure I

KEEP GOING!

could feed my children. As many entrepreneurs know, there are ups and downs - periods of lull and periods of plenty. Well on this occasion, there was a lull. I had spent the entire day making connections and trying to collect some money. It was afternoon, just about time to collect my children from their extracurricular activities, which ended at 5 pm. The school that they attended was near a library. So, I decided to stop by the library in a last-ditch effort to check my email to see if any of my clients had responded favorably.

As it got closer and closer to the time to collect the children, I felt a bit of anxiety creeping in. As soon as they hopped in the truck, they would be hungry, thirsty, tired, and looking to mom for food and drink. This time, I had nothing. There was nothing at home to eat, either. What should I do? Where should I turn? It felt as if every possible avenue was shut off that day.

Psalm 37:25 says, *"I have been young, and now am old; yet have I not seen the righteous forsaken, nor his seed begging bread."* This verse was ever present in my mind. It gave me the confidence that no matter what, I would not have

KEEP GOING!

to ever beg for a meal for my children and I. But it was getting close to 5 o'clock, and nothing had materialized after an entire day of pushing. I was hungry myself, but the needs of my children... the thought of their sweet faces when I collected them from school, overrode my own hunger.

As I drove my truck into the parking lot of the library, I took a deep breath. I have always been a conqueror - facing challenges and overcoming obstacles with vigor. I have had friends and family members that have commented to me that they had no idea I was going through something because I always wear a smile. Some have even asked me how it is that I smile through any storm, adding that they don't think they could have done the same.

In truth, I see life as an adventure. Through the ups and downs, I am always smiling because the good times are so good and the bad times are temporary. Trouble doesn't last always; a popular saying goes.

But on this day, the supermom was a bit discouraged. I had to collect my children soon, and I had no idea what to

KEEP GOING!

tell them. I didn't even have two dollars to buy a gallon of cold water for them.

Still, I had to go into this library and give it one last try. There was no space for a sad or discouraged mother. The children were used to me being exuberant when they saw me after a long day at school. I didn't want this day to be any different, as difficult as it was. My heart was swelling with emotion. I took a deep breath and stepped out of the truck.

On this breezy Autumn day, gusts of wind were twirling around in a funnel. They were lifting leaves and light debris, touching down to the ground and raising back up like jumping beans. It was a beautiful day, and despite what I was going through, I took a moment to admire the beautiful leaves of the Madeira trees swirling around in the parking lot of the library. I looked up to the sky and cried out, "Lord, if you could just bless me with $20 right now to feed my children, Lord. I need you!

At that moment, a wind funnel was hopping by, and a bright, pink Bahamian$20 bill was floating at the top of it! I could not believe my eyes! I looked all around me - to the left

KEEP GOING!

and to the right - to see if the money had belonged to anyone. There was no one else in the parking lot at the time. No one was even near my vicinity. I even looked across the street - not a soul.

Then, I looked at the swirling $20 bill. It was as if I was frozen in time. I was in shock and did not move. But when that pink $20 bill hit the ground and was about to be picked up by another gust of wind, I quickly caught my senses and dashed over and picked it up.

I held that $20 bill in my hands as if it were a million dollars. This was the manifestation of my prayer - instantly! It was unbelievable, but the money was in my hand. It was real. Every bit of anxiety was replaced with a spirit of praise and I started dancing and singing and praising the Almighty God.

I placed the bill in my purse and went into the library. I checked my email, but no one had responded yet. Had I not had that $20 bill, there was a good chance that I might have burst out crying in that library. I would have had to walk out and collect those children with nothing to give them. But instead, I signed out of my email, skipped to my truck, and

KEEP GOING!

went to the grocery store. I was able to buy my children fruit and water for a snack on the way home. I was also able to buy enough groceries to make dinner and give them snacks in their bag for school the next day. The following day brought many blessings, as all the work I put in the day before came to fruition.

I manifested money out of thin air. Scientifically, of course, what happened is that the $20 likely came from another property and was swept away by the wind. Who knows how far it came from in order to land right in my path that day. But there was something supernatural at work. My energy had to be right to line up with all of the energies of the Universe to make the timing perfect for me to receive the money I needed that day, and in that exact moment.

My belief that I would never have to beg for bread; my trust in a power greater than myself; and my faith that makes the impossible possible took over that day. I was in exactly the right place at exactly the right time.

God definitely has a sense of humor. As I stood there in shock, the bill lifted up, about to fly again in another gust

KEEP GOING!

of wind. As I ran to catch the bill, I was laughing. God and I were having a good laugh, as if he were saying to me, "Stay right there not believing your eyes! Now you see it, now you don't!"

Hebrews 11:1 says, *"Now faith is the substance of things hoped for, the evidence of things not seen."* I wholeheartedly believe this to be true - because I have seen it with my own eyes. My faith has manifested much in my life. On this particular day, I manifested what I needed. The $20 was the substance of something hoped for. It was the evidence of the thing I couldn't see before I actually received it. Because when I looked up and asked God for the $20, I knew that He would deliver it. I didn't know how. I didn't know when, but I knew that He would provide.

Even if it was going to be at some later point in the evening, I knew that God would now allow the righteous to beg for bread. We may have just had to wait a bit longer. But I did not have to wait that day. I asked, and it was instantly given. I am not a big asker. I usually attempt to do way too much by myself. In terms of my relationship with God, I was

KEEP GOING!

never an asker. I was always one to give thanks and praise and ask for nothing. But there is a Bible verse that reveals God's promise: "*Ask, and it shall be given to you; seek, and you shall find; knock, and it shall be opened to you.*" - Matthew 7:7. I am learning more and more, the importance of asking.

That $20 has been a reminder to me, all these years later, to KEEP GOING no matter what. The Lord is always with me, seeing me do my best, and girding me with the strength to go on.

The picture of that pink $20 swirling in a flurry of Autumn leaves will forever be etched in my mind. It gives me the inspiration to continue to do my best. My children have been witnesses to many miraculous events in our lives. They have been able to eat and be satisfied from the fruit of my faith. Today, they are loving, intelligent, charismatic adults. They make me so proud. This gives me every reason to keep going!

At this point in my life, I am now working on manifesting a million dollars out of thin air! I am now happily remarried, with two more children, and so in this way, I am

KEEP GOING!

still materializing my blessings, and I have all the more reason to keep going!

If you are a single parent, you know exactly how I felt that Autumn afternoon. You have felt that despair of not knowing where the next dollar was coming from. You know what it is to have a little person or little people depending on you.

Children have the most beautiful eyes.... so innocent and pure. They can melt your heart in a minute. You know that they are depending on you. But please be careful to not translate that responsibility into a burden. You must not let that pressure weigh you down. Give it all to God. Don't forget that you, yourself, are a child. You are a child of your Creator. Oftentimes, we forget that. We think we have no one to turn to. We forget that the One we can turn to is the Creator of us all! You cannot tap into a bigger source than that!

The Bible says to enter the kingdom of God, you must be like a child. Well, time to remember what it's like to be a child! Be happy like a child; be free in spirit like a child; enjoy

KEEP GOING!

nature like a child; forgive like a child; and most importantly - trust like a child.

As a single parent, your child looks up to you for everything. As long as you do not allow negative emotions to affect them, they will be oblivious to what you have to go through to provide them with clothes and shelter. They will be happy every day. They will eat and be satisfied. They will love you unconditionally.

This is what we must do with our Heavenly Father. There He is, waiting on you to trust in Him wholly. He wants you to replace anxiety with happiness. He wants you to be satisfied, no matter your condition, trusting that He is taking on the load and finding the sources of your supply. He is waiting for your unconditional love to manifest in the form of pure faith in Him.

Give your troubles to God! Knowing that He will fuel you in this journey of life, you have every reason to keep going!

KEEP GOING!

"Keep Going"

There is a place no man should go
No woman should venture there
A place confined by a dark abyss
Bound by the depths of despair
It is the land of giving up
Where hopes and dreams, they die
Where the greatest visions are lost in time
And the death of passions lie
This place is no man's land
It bears no fruit for the soul
It is born when the will to win is lost
And life's struggles have taken its toll
So, why give up when no man's land
Can offer you no good vice
When it takes no note of a well-sought goal
And considers not the sacrifice
Lift up your head to heaven's land
The place of prosperity
Never give up on those daring dreams
Keep pushing with sincerity
Keep Going! Keep Going! Don't give up now
The victory is near
Just beyond the toughest trial
Is everything you hold dear
Stand up tall! Face the fight
The battle will be won
Keep Going! Keep Going! The glory is near
And you will be the champion!

KEEP GOING!

Relationships

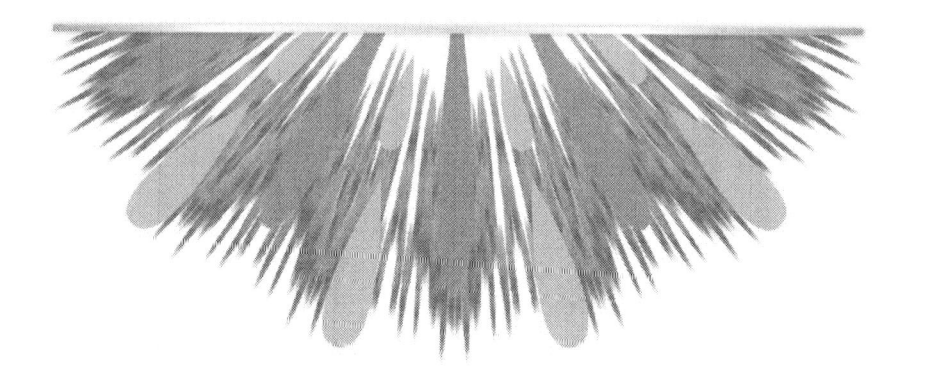

KEEP GOING!

KEEP GOING!

"You Are Not Alone"

Author: Virginia Somerville

If a person believes that they are perfect, they will have no need or motivation to change. They would be satisfied with every aspect of their lives. A person who is down on their luck and penniless with no visible way to better themselves would also believe that their circumstances cannot change. These are two examples that are very different.

The reality is that we are all stuck with the "Who" we think we are supposed to be. Is change possible? Yes, it is indeed. But to make any change, tou must recognize where you are in your life and where you want to be.

Those of us who fall in the middle of the road of life know that change is hard because it is always easier to stay where you are. Call it habit or complacency; old habits are

KEEP GOING!

comfortable. Perhaps this was the way our parents and grandparents lived and thought, and they filtered it down to us and then we possibly passed it along to our children. Now, some generational habits are good things that have positive effects; like learning the importance of family support, prayer, or getting an education. But other habits may have been passed down that need to be changed, however, such as anger, violence, or abuse of any kind.

I, like many others, am a God-fearing woman. This in no way means that I am afraid of God because I cannot be afraid of a God who loves and protects me and provides me with the things I need to sustain my life.

As a woman of God, I am a law-abiding and gracious servant to my family, friends, and community. Not subservient by any means, (I am too opinionated for that!), but I constantly look for ways to serve and improve the lives of those who surround me, in the home, the family, and the community. As Edward Dube states in his book "Beyond the Shade of the Mango Tree," *As we align ourselves with the*

KEEP GOING!

Lord's will, we find that our life gains more meaning. Our motivations change."

Never let the fear of change outweigh the fears that come with progress. You must commit yourself to change to be able to grow and in so doing you should have the support of your caring family and friends. Trust the process, the past doesn't dictate the future. Give yourself permission to make these changes.

You must recognize that a change is needed. It would help you to make a list of the things in your daily life that elicits strong or negative feelings. Remember, all strong feelings are not negative. After making this list go back and put a checkmark by the points that make you feel good. Cross those off your list. Besides the items left put a circle around the ones that you know you can change all by yourself. What's left on your list? They are the negative things that you cannot change. Take these items and write them on a separate sheet of paper. When that is done ask yourself who is the best person to ask to assist you to change these negative items. You will probably find that there are certain items that no one can help

KEEP GOING!

change except the person who created those strong feelings in you. The other items on your list can be worked through with the help of family, friends, or professionals.

These responses will be very different from person to person since no two persons' lives are exactly alike; even though circumstances may be similar. Let's say two couples may be getting a divorce, one divorce could be because of adultery and the other may be because of abuse. Both examples cause emotional trauma, but the details of each will differ drastically.

When you have decided who is best able to assist you with your issues, whether friend, family or professional, you must prioritize the items to the needs of yourself and any others who are involved, usually your children and/or spouse or significant other.

When like-minded people come together and share, everyone comes out smarter. Share your thoughts and ideas with your children. Children think a lot. They have very valid thoughts, ideas, and opinions. Be a good role model, serve your family and others, empathize, and show that you care.

KEEP GOING!

Your family will survive your stumbling through the solo decision making and they will learn to contribute positively as they grow.

"It is not about becoming perfect. It is about the effort you put into the action. When you bring that effort every single day, that is where transformation happens. That is where change occurs." – Author Unknown

Speaking From Experience

A woman, I know personally, (me), was in a situation that required me to change, and my social worker had me do a similar exercise. My husband was active-duty military and had physically abused our 2 sons and sexually abused our 3 daughters. My list was long, and I narrowed it down to the things I couldn't change about my situation. I had to recognize that even though I was feeling extreme guilt about the circumstances that I had no control over, the items remaining on my list could only be changed by my husband and he wasn't willing to do so.

KEEP GOING!

During my marriage, I truly loved my husband and catered to his every need, so when his abuse of our children came to light, I was in shock and denial. I then questioned myself as to why I hadn't seen signs of these things happening. Surely there had been some hints or signals that this was going on. When I confronted my husband, he denied all accusations.

One night I called a helpline and was referred to a counselor. The next day the counselor requested I take the older children from school and bring them into her office where she talked with them individually. Then she made a few phone calls and requested I take the children and go to a facility run by the state and someone would bring my two younger children to meet us there. While I waited to speak to someone official, the city police brought my two little kids to me and we were shown into a comfortable room with a couple of stuffed chairs and a couch and lots of toys and books.

There I found out that my husband had been arrested on child abuse charges and jailed in the military base where he remained until after his sentencing. Since my husband was in the military, he was arrested by the Military Police, jailed

KEEP GOING!

on base, held, and charged with child abuse. His case could not be heard in a civilian court and had to go before a Military Tribunal for sentencing.

What this meant was that my children and I had to be represented by a military lawyer and I was required to bring all 5 of my children to the court every single day of the trial in case the Tribunal wished to ask them any questions. Thankfully, they did not have to be in the courtroom; a close family friend was allowed to sit with the children in another room. But nonetheless, it was a horrible, emotional, and stressful ordeal to endure. Ours was the first child abuse case ever heard in a Military Court.

After the sentencing, the reality of this new change started to sink in as I discovered how many other decisions had to be made. I created a whole new list with a new set of items to be prioritized, the majority of which centered around my children. My priorities had changed. The decisions were no longer about just myself. I now had to make all decisions on my own. Would I have to move from military housing? How would I pay bills and car expenses? The questions went

KEEP GOING!

on and on. I had never done a budget on my own. Whom could I turn to for advice and counseling?

At first, I panicked. How, why, where, and when? The thoughts kept me up at night. They plagued me during the daylight hours. I wanted to run screaming into the night and never come back. But then I walked the halls and looked into the bedrooms at my sleeping children. My babies. I knew then and there that running away was not the answer. I had to find a way to cope and to help us all survive.

We all find ourselves changing our priorities. It is part of the progression in this journey called life! Remember the adage that you can never sit still; if you are not moving forward, then you are moving backward. I hate the feeling of retreating. It's like admitting I failed. The important thing to remember is that you pick yourself up. Then you look ahead and decide that today will have at least one positive thing occur, even if it is as simple as getting out of bed and brushing your teeth and dressing for the day.

We all feel like we let someone down but try to remember that everyone else has the same feelings. You are

KEEP GOING!

not alone in this. For me, my life is centered around prayer. Not so formalized as praying only during dedicated times, but my prayer life is a running dialog throughout the day that is like "Father, I really need you" for whatever is happening at that moment. Or it could be that a friend or family member asks to be remembered in my prayers. If I wait until bedtime, I will probably forget the details they had wanted to be included in the prayer.

I have always been grateful for my belief in a God that would support and sustain me through all my trials and in all my joys. I had the support of my Bishop at church, and many friends and family. But there were also many trials from many friends and family because they were sure that I was at fault somehow. I was ostracized, shunned, and excluded from many activities, as were my beautiful, innocent children. Many times, the children were not invited to play, or to friends' birthday parties and activities.

I personally, do not understand those people who have closed minds and cannot tell the difference between the victims and the perpetrator. From then until now, I shake my

KEEP GOING!

head at the injustice placed upon a family who was trying to put the pieces of their lives into a semblance of normal on the surface and to heal within with the support of those who understood the drama, grief, and struggles they would experience for years to come. Intolerance and injustice survive amidst all the good that people can do for each other. It shows up in small and insidious ways to plague and torment the innocent.

My five children and I were homeless for nearly a year and passed through many homeless shelters where we were well taken care of but had rules that limited the amount of time we could spend in each residence. We never went hungry, and we always had clothing in good condition to wear. We were always crammed into a "family room" that was designed for 4 people, and we were a family of 6.

Yet throughout it all, I made sure that no matter where we were that I took my children to church. We shared our feelings and concerns as to the occurrences of the day and how they felt about jumping from school to school during that year,

KEEP GOING!

even though the youngest two did not always understand what that meant.

A friend once told me, "In math, a negative + a negative equal a positive, but a negative mind will never give you a positive." I always remember this wisdom because we are required to learn to make many types of changes in a lifetime. You did not learn to tie your shoes and then stop learning for the rest of your life. Learning is ongoing. Part of learning and growth is sharing your time, talents, and energy with those around you. But at the same time, you must allow others to serve you.

Yes, it seems embarrassing and difficult but just think of how happy you make those who do some small service for you. As an example, I "allow" my sister to sweep a floor or wash a dish when she visits because it makes her feel like she is contributing to easing my day. I didn't always allow others to do things for me because I was "capable. I am sure that you, too, can relate to this - right?!

There are unlimited possibilities within each of us. I have tried to teach my children this principle over their

KEEP GOING!

lifetimes. With some, I was more successful than with others. How many times do I remember my own mother cautioning me to stop doing this and you should be doing that. We have all had at least one person in our lives that we considered a "nagger", not realizing at the time the wisdom that they are trying to share with us.

Now that my children have all moved on with their lives I am so pleased with their decisions and where they have allowed themselves to grow and develop. One works with computers, another is an elementary school teacher, one lives in Japan and runs an international school. Another became a Master Reiki Healer, and my youngest became a mom. Now, I offer advice occasionally but I do not find it necessary to tell anyone they must, or that they should say or do something. It is a relief and a joy to watch my grandchildren grow and expand their lives and careers as well.

Individually, each of us has complex and sometimes complicated lives filled with joy, pleasures, sadness, and pain. Where we focus our attention is the direction we will travel on our individual roads. If you focus on the positive then your

KEEP GOING!

outcomes will almost always be positive. It is not to say there will not be problems, because there definitely will be, but moving through those problems with a positive goal in sight will be worth the effort it takes to get there.

A note I made in a seminar some time ago says "Where are you right now? Love your family. Stay committed to God. Continue improving myself and continue walking upward. Share and serve my neighbors and live closer to my family." As notes go, there was probably a lot more said but those were the things I found relevant. A reminder to myself to focus on the good I can do every day.

Where do you want to go? Who do you want to travel this path with? Who will you serve along the way? How grateful are you for the journey you are on? Do you appreciate the road with all its' twists and turns?

My journey in life has been up and down, left and right, and sometimes has had roadblocks. These roadblocks are sometimes of my own doing and sometimes are challenges that have been placed in my way that I must find a way around.

KEEP GOING!

But always, I have found that my emotional support and strength have come to me through study, prayer, and thoughtful contemplation of all aspects of my journey. I have created a Gratitude journal, (which I admittedly do not write in every day), but sometimes it is as simple as, "Today I woke up refreshed". Even the smallest of children can make a picture with paper and crayons of what makes them happy. It is very enlightening. Try it.

Gratitude is free. It costs us nothing but recognition, but it is very liberating to voice these things in recognition of God's love and caring hand watching over us all the days of our lives.

I have great love and appreciation for those family and friends who have always stood by and supported my children and me in our many struggles. I am very grateful for my children who bore with all my mistakes and sometimes clumsy attempts to keep them safe and happy.

Here is a parting thought, *"Real love is not based on romance, candlelight dinners, and long walks on the beach. It is based on respect, compromise, care, and trust."* (Author

KEEP GOING!

unknown). Remember, we are human, we all make mistakes. Keep your chin up, and your eyes looking heavenward, and always remember that you are loved, and you are never alone. And as Walt Disney said: "Keep Moving Forward."

KEEP GOING!

Resilience & Perseverance

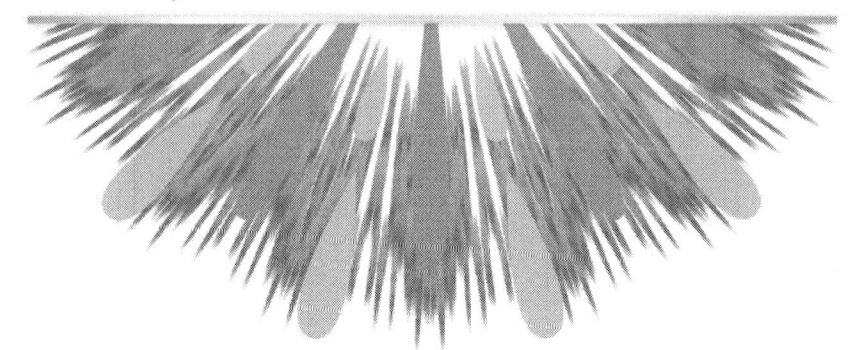

KEEP GOING!

KEEP GOING!

"Push Purposefully"

Author: Krista Barr-Bastian

Life is indeed a journey. As with any journey, there are mountains and valleys. However, we must learn that neither the mountain nor the valley should be considered in isolation. Instead, they are all a part of bigger, wider, deeper picture - a beautiful rendition of the faithfulness of God manifesting as purpose in our lives. Each season of your life is critically important to the plan of God. It is therefore imperative that you fasten your faith in God so that you can PUSH through it all and step into the promise of God.

I have come to learn that God is very strategic - I call him "Master Orchestrator". Everything that you encounter in life- whether good or bad- is a building block to the promises

KEEP GOING!

of God over your life. It is a necessary step on the path to the place of promise, where you are most purposeful and fruitful.

My life was simple and perfect until my early twenties. I began to experience valleys during my marriage which occurred in my mid-twenties. It was about two weeks prior to my wedding in the chaos of last-minute finalizations that I decided to ask God if this marriage was what He really wanted for me. I remember feeling that God was giving me the "silent treatment". At that moment I knew that I was in for an adventure; I knew that this marriage would present itself as the "refiner"- and it did!

The marriage never seemed to get its grounding- it stayed rocky. The more I attempted to tighten my grip on it – the more life applied the pressure; prying one finger off at a time until the complete hold was released. I found myself separated after six short yet long years of marriage with four young kids- the youngest was just two weeks old. I remember facing the reality of being in a home alone with four kids – two under two- after my husband so willingly walked away in pursuit of his freedom. The tiles of my living room floor knew

KEEP GOING!

my story well; they collected the tears of a broken heart and hopeless soul.

But this had to be endured, it was a part of the journey. It was here that I began to look to God for strength. I was also very blessed to have my mother walk alongside me to help me adjust to my new normal. But, two years after the separation, my mother suddenly became sick and took her final rest. Her and my grandmother passed away a week apart.

I was left alone. No hand to hold. No one by my side. Yet again, a new normal that I had to endure…this time alone. I wanted to pity myself and cry endlessly. But God kept calling me with a voice of authority out of the self-pity and into purpose. He was calling me to PUSH through it all. He was commanding me to Keep Going.

But how could I keep going in the mess that was my life? I felt desolate and burdened. Being a single mother of four "vibrant" kids had me stretched emotionally, physically, and financially. It was all overwhelming, but God was calling me to make moves in this mess. I couldn't comprehend it. It truly made no sense to me. Why would you want to use me in

KEEP GOING!

a state like this? Don't you want to wait until I can get things under control and in some good form? This is when I began to understand that God is not a God of perfection, but He gets glory when He can use imperfection for His good purpose. So, as much as my pain wanted to stagnate and stifle me, I had to make the move by faith- I had to PUSH; I had to keep going – lonely, hurting, tired, and all.

God was calling me to write a book, particularly for women, about emerging out of trials purposefully. I was at first reluctant for several reasons; I was uncertain about my writing skills; I was still trying to get through my own trials- so who was I to write a book to tell others how to and I didn't want to use the level of financial resources required of me to write and publish a book.

However, in obedience, I obliged. I realized that the only way out of this was taking the steps ordered by God in faith. Further, I understood the vision that God had given to me over my life, and I was convinced that these steps were a pivotal part of the birth of that vision. So, I kept going.

KEEP GOING!

I don't know the intricacies of where you may be right now in your life or what you are faced with at this very moment. However, I want you to know that before you do anything else you must be clear on the vision that God has for your life. To keep going you must have some idea of where you are designed to go. God has woven you into the lives of so many others. These people are depending on you to continue to PUSH- to continue to follow the steps ordered by God.

As you know, to give natural birth to a baby you must PUSH! However, pushing only begins when the contractions come to a "boiling point". It is then in great pain that the woman's body has the unquenching urge to push in order to move the baby along the birthing canal where it crowns and then is ultimately pushed all the way out.

The same applies to the vision of God over your life. During some of the most difficult and challenging seasons in your life, God is going to make a call on you to PUSH. This means He wants you to make a move that is in alignment with His plan for your life. That move may seem nonsensical given

KEEP GOING!

the reality that you are in. But you will have to close your eyes and move with your faith and get it done! Just keep going! This is the only way that you will see the fullness of the vision attached to your name show up on the earth.

Just as the desire to push in natural birth comes with a physical urge - the spiritual push to birth your purpose is accompanied by a deeply rooted urge as well- it will stand strong in your spirit calling for your immediate attention. No matter your circumstance- keep going and make the move. PUSH by faith!

There are five PUSH Principles that God has revealed to me and that I want to share with you. Once you ground yourself in these principles, they will expand your faith and allow for a stronger PUSH through the difficult seasons of life- it will help you to preserve powerfully and keep going.

POWERFUL PERSON

It is important that you know your identity in God. You are a child of God made in his image and likeness. You need to remember this as you traverse the valleys of life. This

KEEP GOING!

allows you to walk through your trials with an uncommon authority and affords you the confidence to keep going. Please understand that there is certainty in your identity. Therefore, the "who you are" does not change with circumstances.

Your identity is not about your occupation, your place of residence, your citizenship, your marital status, or your possessions. These things can change. The truth of who you are is stable and constant- it never changes. Genesis 1:26-27 tells us *"God created mankind in his own image, in the image of God he created them; male and female he created them"*. This is your creative design, and this doesn't change.

Like God, you were created with the ability to rule. He has given you a presence of power and a capacity of mind to have dominion in the earth. You must come to know how powerful you are as a child of God. This knowledge will empower you to- keep going!

POWERFUL PURPOSE

You are anointed and appointed! Jeremiah 1:5 states *"Before I formed you in the womb I knew you, before you were*

KEEP GOING!

born, I set you apart; I appointed you as a prophet to the nations." Yes! There is a unique and particular purpose over your life and you must cross every valley to get there.

There are people on the other side waiting to be "delivered" by the fruit of you. Their lives depend on you! They are praying that you endure the trials of life and birth the very purpose within you that is meant to save their lives.

You must keep going for "your people"! You are their light. You are critical to their prosperity. They are waiting on you, don't leave them in the dark- keep going!

POWERFUL PRESENCE

You cannot walk the trials of life alone. You must get in the presence of God. This is how you keep going. God has given you the great gift of His Holy Spirit, the great advocate, to help you push powerfully along the journey of life. The Holy Spirit strengthens you as you dwell in the word of God, commit to prayer, live a life of continual praise no matter your circumstances, and constantly declare the promises of God over your life.

KEEP GOING!

Hebrews 13:5 tells us that the Lord will never leave you nor never forsake you. Get into the disciple of magnifying the presence of God in your life. You are not alone! You can endure all that life presents before you with the strength that comes from the Holy Spirit. Create space for the Spirit of God to dwell deeply within and around you and – keep going!

POWERFUL PERSPECTIVE

Your mindset is very important as you endure the tough times of life. You have got to be convinced that everything you face will work for the good purposes of God no matter how bad it appears. Further, you must realize that we are humans who are bound by space and time and are not privy to the bigger plan of God. Hence, we cannot lean on our own understanding we must be intentional about trusting God with our steps.

So many times, we try to control the narrative of our lives. We are disappointed when situations aren't shaping up to our plans. Proverbs 19:21 says *"Many are the plans in a person's heart, but it is the Lord's purpose that will prevail."* As you PUSH your way through know that God has the events

KEEP GOING!

of your life purposeful and in perfect sequence and all things will work for your good. This is the right mindset you need to keep going!

POWERFUL PATIENCE

There is a time and a season for everything. That includes seasons of trial and disruptions and seasons of prosperity and promise. You must endure your season of difficulties before you can step into your place of promise and fullness of purpose. Remember, before a baby is born there is tremendous pain that a mother must endure before her final push which releases the baby entirely from her womb.

We also know that labor times vary. There is no set time frame. We can only be patient and continue to push; continue to keep going. You must have confidence in the fact that there is an appointed time for you to be ushered from a "place of suffering" to a "place of fruitfulness". You must wait on this time.

Time is in the ultimate control of God, and we know that He does all things well and He is always on time. This

KEEP GOING!

gives us the peace to be patient no matter how arduous our circumstances may become. Habakkuk 2:3 tells us that though the vision lingers, WAIT for it. You will emerge purposeful. God has promised you that he has a plan for you to give you hope and a future...be patient and -keep going!

Keep PUSHING Through!

I implore you to consider these principles in your daily living and PUSH through every tough season of your life and see the emergence of the beauty of God's promise for you. The troubles you are feeling right now are contractions; indicating that you are birthing something magnificent on behalf of heaven. Don't give up now, keep going...PUSH!!!!

There is purpose within you. You are carrying a fruit that is needed on the earth. The world needs the fullness of you; your life is so much bigger than you. There are many whose lives depend on yours; many whose purpose is connected to your purpose.

You are pivotal to the plan of God! Stand with authority in the valley! Have the audacity to reign and have

KEEP GOING!

dominion amid life's struggles. YOU ARE A CHILD OF GOD! Walk like it, talk like it, be it!

Will you push with me? I am pushing right now! In the chaos of my life, I am showing up and doing what God has so commanded me to do. Sometimes that looks like crying because of the woes of single motherhood and wiping through tears to show up on stages and platforms that look to me to impart inspiration.

Sometimes it looks like sitting in front of my laptop; my body struck weak with COVID but punching the keys to get the message out to a people God has attached to my "womb".

Whatever it may be for you, you've got to show up anyways; in the mess and imperfections- just as you are! Keep going where God has sent you and keep doing what He is telling you to do.

Whatever you do, promise me you won't stop PUSHING!

KEEP GOING!

"When Strength Was All I Knew"

Author: Olivia Munroe Fergus

"Where there is no struggle, there is no strength"

Traveling on my life journey, I was met with so many obstacles that could have hindered me from progressing in life. Instead of laying down and playing dead, I stood up and kept on fighting, and every obstacle was used for my advantage.

My Starting Point

I grew up in a comfortable environment with both parents and two sisters, where I was always provided for. Being the last out of the bunch, I was spoiled but disciplined. However, that comfortable home was abruptly taken from under me without a warning.

KEEP GOING!

Sadly, my mom and dad departed which left me to be raised by a single parent and on a different island from where we once lived. This was the beginning of the emotional trauma in my life. Moreover, I was young, hurt, confused, and now living in a shattered world. I was already accustomed to a certain lifestyle and living with a smaller family.

Unfortunately, it wasn't the same when we relocated to be with my grandmother. We were now living with a larger family and a reduced space. The worst part of it, my father was practically absent from life. But even though the beginning of relocating was uncomfortable, contentment settled in. Living with my grandmother, many life lessons were learned. She was an exceptional role model in my life.

My "Grammy" was my world. She was my "Mum" and I was her "Lydia". I found my peace and comfort just being around her. While my mother was so busy being a provider, my grandmother played the role of the nurturer.

Strength was all she knew. My grandmother taught me how to be strong by the way she demonstrated and also shared her life stories on how she handled challenges. She was a

KEEP GOING!

strong-minded woman, who sought to progress in life. She never "cried over spilled milk", she made things happen with or without the help of others. She was a very determined and self-driving woman.

Growing up in The Bahamas, on the island of Exuma in the settlement of Richmond's Hill, my grandmother was taught at a very young age about entrepreneurship. Her father owned a farm that she attended to before heading off to school and after. Early morning rises and long walking was her routine almost every day to ensure that her morning chores were done on the farm. She was very dedicated and active on her dad's farm.

While her other siblings left home to begin their own journeys of life, she stayed in Exuma and continued helping her father with the farm. As tedious as that might have seemed, she did it. She later dropped out of school at age thirteen to be a full caretaker of the farm because her help was required. Social life or having friends was something my grandmother never really had.

KEEP GOING!

Normally in her era, at the age of thirteen is when courtship would have started, marriage, and then having children. Well, my grandmother was late to all of that.

She got married at the age of twenty-eight and had her first child at twenty-nine. By that time, she was already financially established with two businesses (farming chicken and being a straw vendor). She was so focused on what she wanted. While she was missing out on enjoying life, she was trying to start a stable foundation for her children.

Moreover, those businesses were able to take care of her along with her husband while she was being fruitful in bearing her children. She was so fruitful in her child-bearing stage that she stopped at the age of forty-five and had twelve children. An awesome mother was she to both her children and grandchildren.

Growing up in most families, the grandparents' home was always the place to be. My grandmother's home was the place everybody had a chance to live. She welcomed everyone with open arms. Provision was made for everyone, big and small.

KEEP GOING!

Additionally, I have been very active in my grandmother's life, so I was able to experience firsthand the great mom she was.

In all of my years, I haven't ever seen my grandmother show any emotional distress or fret over anything. She was always in a calm praying state. Her strength encouraged me to be strong through adversity. Anytime I would have wanted a sound council, I would reach out to her. A wise counselor she was to me. She always directed me to God to get a clear answer. If faith was a person, it would have been her. She taught me to trust God in and with everything. From her perspective, no one needed to know what you are going through in your home just God alone. What you don't have God will provide.

Change is a hard process to endure. My mom decided that we now needed our own place, so we relocated. After leaving my grandmother, I felt a little distraught because I was leaving my happy place. She ensured whenever I came to visit her, I wouldn't leave out empty-handed or without a little pocket change to put in my hand. She would reach right into

KEEP GOING!

her bosom and unfold a brown paper where she kept her money and said "here gal, don't tell anybody". I have watched my grandmother stand her ground in many situations that would have swept a weak person away. I have watched her pull herself together when "all hell was breaking loose in her life". She did whatever she could to keep her family together.

She was widowed at the age of 65. At that time, she had two of her children in college. Her provider was no longer there but the bills had to be paid. She had no time to have a pity party or wait for a handout. She pushed her businesses and made sure everything was in place for them. The tenacity she had was incredible. The shoes she left behind are big ones to fill. She gave me great insight on becoming an awesome mother to my children and an entrepreneur. When I am faced with difficulties, she taught me that I had one option and that is to fight it through.

The Becoming

You can say "I am tough like an old boot". The situations I faced at a young age and still encounter today tried to break me but weren't successful. I came upon a speed

KEEP GOING!

bump early during my own journey in life. When I first found out I was pregnant with my daughter I was terrified because I didn't know how to face my mother. My dad, I wasn't too afraid of but I knew he would have been disappointed. But the real fear was for my mother. My heart leaped out of my chest when she found out, she was furious. I thank God at that time I was pregnant.

Then, a sense of shame and embarrassment came over me when the rest of my family found out. Many might congratulate you but only a hand full of people meant it and for the others, you are just a hot topic. I had a dear aunt who called me and pacified me with comforting words. She said to me life happens but you will surpass it.

The worse part of it all, I was upset and disappointed in my daughter's dad because this wasn't supposed to be a one-man's journey in raising her. While he had the option to be actively involved as a parent, I didn't. It was more nerve-wracking to me than anything. Not only that he was rarely a part of her life, but without his full involvement I couldn't really pursue the dream career I sought to do directly out of

KEEP GOING!

school. Complications presented themselves during my pregnancy with my daughter which caused an early delivery due to the signs of preeclampsia. She was also born asthmatic.

Can you imagine? A young teenage mom with a sickly baby. I was just wrapping my head around becoming a mother and now I had to face the reality of having to be a mom with a sickly baby. I can remember having to catch the bus to the clinic and rushing her straight onto the oxygen tank. It was a struggle because she hated putting on the mask.

On one hand, I hated to hear the cry of discomfort from my baby, and on the other hand, I wanted her to get well. Traveling to the ER and the clinic by myself really had me emotionally drained and tired. I had many sleepless nights watching her sleep because I was scared of the way she was breathing. It wasn't easy at all but we made it through.

I can recall her dad's mom inviting me to church one Sunday and after church, she stopped at a plaza and found a young tree. She marked my baby under the tree and said as this grows so will asthma grow out of your baby.

KEEP GOING!

The older generation is very superstitious. I really didn't believe in it and believed more in the power of prayer but I must say she doesn't have asthma anymore after growing up.

Furthermore, I wasn't just dealing with being there for my baby emotionally and physically, I had to also be there financially. Do you know what it is to hear people telling you how the father of your child is living their best life when you are struggling to meet the needs of you and your child?

Many question me on how did I manage to keep it together? My response was but God. I thank God for the few friends I had in my life. When situations seemed gloomy like there was no way out, God always provided. I might not have complained too much but I cried out to God. He always provided. I had times I couldn't afford pampers and turning to family was harder than turning to a stranger. I had my share of disappointment but I manage to pull myself up.

I remembered every word my grammy said to me. That is why it is important to surround yourself with people who

KEEP GOING!

truly care about you, and whose words will continue to comfort you even when they aren't around.

Having my daughter Keianna didn't stop my plans it just detoured me in a different direction for the time being. One thing I knew for sure is that I didn't want to be such a busy parent trying to provide for my child that I would lose the connection with her.

My dream career ever since I was a child was to be a lawyer and I know it takes a lot of time away from everything because it requires plenty researching and reading. Nevertheless, I worked in a salon and other secretarial jobs until I got tired and opened up a beauty supply store and salon named after her (Keke's Beauty Supplies & Notions).

I had already experienced what it was like to be without my mother at home because she had to work so hard to keep bills paid. I refused to take that same route with my child and the other children I had.

At times, I did feel guilty because I knew I could have done more with my life but I always heard that young voice

KEEP GOING!

speaking to me saying mommy I need you to be home with me. Don't get me wrong, I enjoyed every part of being home to nurture, guide and provide for my child.

Gratitude is the Attitude! Through everything, my child turned out to be an exceptional child. She graduated from high school on the principal's list, started college and during her first semester she obtained a 4.00 g.p.a and started two successful companies.

In addition, I had two other children and was blessed with two bonus children. All of this paved the way for me to be a remarkable mother. I had to go through various stages to become a healthier version of myself. I might not be a perfect mother but I try my hardest to be a good one. Just as I was instilled with morals and standards, the baton was passed on to them.

My journey drew me closer to God, taught me how to forgive, and how to let go of all my excess baggage, and it gave me the attitude of gratitude. *"When we learn how to become resilient, we learn how to embrace the beautiful broad spectrum of human experience."* ~ Unknown Author

KEEP GOING!

Uncovering the Mystery to Healing

One may ask, how did I do it? How did you manage, to pick yourself up every time life seems to present some difficult task your way? I sometimes wonder for myself how I was able to make it through some of the very hard times that I endured. I thank God for the life principles my late grandmother once taught me and will forever live in me.

Firstly, I learned to put my trust in God. When I became overwhelmed and confused, I found myself drawing closer to Him through praying, worshipping, and reading my bible.

I was very tight lipped on what I was going through because of shame. I hid my pain away from others so they could have believed everything was okay but deep down I wasn't. You might be secretly fighting a battle, but once you release it all to Him at your vulnerable moment, He will strengthen you.

Through secretly praying to God, He rewarded me openly with favor and healed me. Secondly, gratitude is

KEEP GOING!

essential! Sometimes, the bad might seem to be so prevalent in life but if we take the time to acknowledge the good, we would see how privileged and blessed we really are.

Complain less and stay positive. It won't be easy but give it a try. When I started focusing on what God was doing for me in the midst of my tribulation, I became more positive and grateful. Moreover, I watched situations turn around for my good. Even though it felt like I was on a lonely journey, God sent angels from all avenues to assist me with the rearing of my child.

He says, as your praises go up the blessings will come down. In my life, I have found that to not just be a saying but reality. You have to be practical and consistent with gratification.

Thirdly, you have to forgive. Forgiveness is the key to any hurt you might be experiencing. That process is very tedious. Many might think that just by saying you forgive someone that is it. Well, they are wrong. Forgiveness requires more mental work and soul searching. Take time with yourself in meditation to get to the root cause of the problem.

KEEP GOING!

By doing so, you can confront your issues and self-heal. Remember forgiveness isn't about the person but it's for you. You have to let go of all excess baggage to enjoy your future. There is a lesson in every hurt. Make it a point to find out what it is, so that you can learn from it and move on in a positive way with your life.

KEEP GOING!

"Your Faith Has Healed You"

Author: Tashoy Walters

We were created to live a happy, healthy, loving, and prosperous life. Sometimes, that is not always the case. As much as we desire to live an EASY life, we cannot help that outside circumstances will cause us to want to give up! Being heartbroken can cripple you, grieving a death of a loved one, losing a job, house, car, friendship, or marriage. You name it! There are times in our life when we can and or will be faced with challenges that we have to decide if we are still going to live this "thing" called life.

Take a moment and look at your life and see all the things you have survived! You should be proud of yourself! I am going to give you a perspective and encouragement from a biblical view of how you were able to make it this far and

KEEP GOING!

how you will continue to keep going no matter the circumstance.

Your faith is what healed you, your faith (confidence and trust in The Father and yourself) is what carried you through. Let me tell you a bible story you can find in the New Testament Luke 8. I am sharing it from a perspective that will relate to us TODAY.

There was a woman who had a lot of issues. Issues that she carried for a very, very, very long time. Issues that she didn't tell anyone because it was personal; between her and God. She dealt with depression, sadness, suicidal thoughts, loneliness, low self-esteem, death, daddy issues, mother issues, childhood trauma, jealousy, and body image issues, you name it. For many years she carried these hidden mental and emotional secrets. No one knew because she carried herself so well. She was well put together externally but internally she was dark, angry, malicious, and depressed. She held these issues close to her and did not want anyone to know. But she knew that one day she would be completely healed. She persevered; she pushed through. She made up her

KEEP GOING!

mind that one day all these issues and the bags that she carried would one day, be gone.

For years, she went to therapists, and they helped her on the surface, but they did not connect with her soul. She needed something deeper! She knew by faith (confidence in The Father and Self) she would be healed.

One early morning, she decided that despite all the issues she carried she will be released from it all and be FREE. She knew she would be healed. She heard about a healer that was coming to her area. She heard of all the great things that would happen at the conferences, workshops, and services. So, she decided to see this healer that everybody was raving about.

She drove about six hours to see him and when she finally got to her destination, she was amazed at all the people that we there and around The Healer. There were so many people around this one man that she felt discouraged and wanted to turn back. But then she thought to herself "what if I believed (trust and be confident) in myself to make my way to the front touch him and leave," she thought to herself again,

KEEP GOING!

this might be my only chance of being completely healed. The Healer had people press around him from all sides, everybody was around him.

So, she decided I am going in and she pressed her way. She pushed her way through everybody she passed through. She crawled over people. She crawled under. She pressed on and she moved forward.

"Excuse me, please I need to get through." she said "I need to see this great healer this great man, excuse me, please." And she pressed her way forward. It took her another two hours to get to him. Right when she was so close to him, she said to herself, "You know what, I just need to touch him. There's a small piece of his clothing. Because if he is able to heal these people, I know if I just touch him, I would be healed". And then she was so close to him that she was able to touch just a little string of his garment and then this great healer turned around and said "Somebody touched me". Everybody else looked around him and said, well duh, it's like a thousand people here that are touching you! But The Healer said "This is a particular touch. Somebody touched me." He

KEEP GOING!

then looked at the woman and deep in her soul she knew he was meaning her. As they locked eyes, the great healer smiled at the woman and said, "Woman, your FAITH has healed you".

Now let's refocus on you. Your faith is where the perseverance lies, your faith is where resilience lies. You must exercise your faith. You must make a decision and decide today to believe everything is working out for you, and accept that God is within you, and *you will not fail*. Just like this woman with her issue she carried for many years and one day she decided I am going to use my faith to heal myself. The great healer did not say I healed you. He said, Woman your FAITH has healed you.

Your faith can heal you. But you must walk by faith and not by sight. All you need is a mustard seed of faith. The bible says all you need is a mustard seed of faith to move a mountain. Go ahead and go look up a picture of a mustard seed and go look up Mount Everest. Your mustard seeds of faith can move that big problem. Your mustard seed of faith can get you from low self-esteem to high confidence. Your mustard

KEEP GOING!

seed of faith can get you from depression to joy. Your mustard seeds of faith can get you from broke to multimillionaire, your mustard seed of faith can get you from single to happily married, your mustard seed of faith can make you get you the promotion, your mustard seed of faith is what you need!

The belief and faith that you need is found within you. God is within you, and you shall not fail. In life, all sorts of things can happen to us; relationships can hurt us; jobs can fail us; we can fail ourselves. Humans can fail us but the love of God never fails. And the one thing that we should not allow to fail us is our own faith in ourselves!

Even if you are at a place in your life that is turbulent and not comfortable, and you may feel like you want to stop going, thi is the time where you need to use your belief of being sure of who you are. When you are sure of yourself, sure of who you are or sure and who your belief is in, you will never have to worry about the outcome of any challenge.

When you are sure that your prayers are going to be answered despite what things may look or feel like, you will see and feel a brighter day. To be sure means to be confident

KEEP GOING!

and to know that you are grounded in who you are. That is the keep to keep moving forward. That's the key to not stopping.

Yes, sometimes the things in life may want to break us down. We can pause for a moment; it's okay to pause. It's okay to take a break. It's okay to take that time alone. It's okay to take time to heal. It's okay to take time to rest. But what we don't do is stop. The only thing that we stop doing is anything that hurts us and does not bring us joy, anything that will cause trauma and may keep us away from what we are supposed to fulfilled in on this earth. That's what we stop. To keep going you have to be sure in who you are. Once you get the baseline of certainty, nothing, no one, can get in your way.

We may think it is always all about us doing it alone in reality, we are not meant to live alone. We are not meant to fight all our battles alone. I want you ask yourself right now, who can I go to if I can no longer push myself?

Right now, we are going to take a another look at perseverance and resistance from a biblical perspective and relate it to today's time. Luke 5: 17 – 32 talks about when Jesus was in this house, and it was packed. There were so

KEEP GOING!

many people there that needed to be healed. There was a lame man that could not walk, and some people brought him on a stretcher. But guess what? They could not get into the home because it was so filled with so many people. These people who brought the man on the stretcher knew that if they brought him to Jesus, he will be healed. Do you know what these guys did? They climbed on top of the roof with the lame man in this stretcher, found out where Jesus was and lowered him down to Jesus. And when they did this Jesus, saw their confidence in him springing from their faith, he said, man, Your sins are forgiven.

The scribes and the Pharisees began to complain and whisper amongst themselves, saying "Who is this man"? "No one can forgive sins but God alone". But Jesus knew their thoughts and questions so he answered them. "Why do you question in your hearts, which is easier to say: 'Your sins are forgiven or to say arise and walk'? "But that you may know that the Son of Man has the power of authority and the right on earth to forgive", so he said to the paralyzed man, "I say to you, rise, pick up your stretcher and go to your own house".

KEEP GOING!

And instantly, the man stood up before them and picked up what he'd been laying on and went away to his house recognizing and praising and thanking God.

Now I asked you this question. When you need to heal and you are paralyzed, and you can no longer move, either physically, mentally or spiritually, who is going to carry you? Who is going to carry you and stand in the gap, to be able to make sure that you get your healing?

Our battles that we fight should not be fought alone. And it's very unfortunate that today we live in a society that encourages and celebrates the attitude of "It's me and me, all by myself. No new friends." That is a wrong and dangerous perspective. We all need a tribe. We all need a sister. We all need a brother. We all need that therapist; we all need someone that can help us when we cannot help ourselves.

There are times when we have to do it alone, but sometimes our issues and our weight can be so heavy that we become paralyzed and we cannot move. I ask you again. Who will carry you to the great healer when you cannot heal

KEEP GOING!

yourself. That's a question that I will leave with you to ask yourself.

If you can name two people, you are blessed if you are able to name one person you are blessed if you are able to name zero people you are still blessed. But if you are in the category or situation where you feel that you do not have anyone like that, I highly encourage you that you use your faith in yourself and in God and ask God for someone who walks in love, and who will be able to carry you when you need it, or need a friend.

We all need that love. We all need that tribe to help us when we cannot help ourselves. Yes, God is very able. He also created each one of us to love each other. My mentor Cathy Robinson Pickett has a saying, "Hand in hand we all can make a difference. Hand in hand we all can pull each other up hand in hand, we all can love each other". She also gave me an analogy that we all have a rope and at the end of the rope, there is a knot and sometimes we are at the end of our rope, who is going to pull you up.

KEEP GOING!

Stay Encouraged

I hope after you have read this chapter, you are encouraged, and I was able to help you use the Word of God to activate your faith and help reconnect you to God that is within you. I want you to remember these 3 things:

1. You will not fail
2. Your faith is what will carry you.
3. You should be very happy and proud of where you are right now. This is important. I want you to celebrate everything that you have gone through, and celebrate where you at. You should celebrate being in this time, space, and reality in this physical body that you are here, and you made it through.
4. I also want you to reflect and see if you have a tribe who will carry you when you need it. Just like we just read in Luke chapter five. That is such a powerful Scripture. And even myself I have used it to make sure that I have at least one or two people that when I am at my low and I put pride aside, I can be completely

KEEP GOING!

transparent as myself. I love on God and have God in the physical and people to love on me.

God bless you and I hope you have been pulled up and your faith has been activated and you know how to keep going and persevere.

Spirituality

KEEP GOING!

KEEP GOING!

"God's Peace"

Author: Alicia Hernandez

To say that there will come a time when life's hardships will cease to exist, at least in this life, would be a lie. Every season of life will yield new challenges, trials, tribulations, and sorrows. This fact is inescapable. There are some circumstances we can change, and others we cannot but the one thing we can always change is our response, and our perspective. I don't say these things to discourage or dismay, but rather to offer hope and a clear view of how to best navigate these challenges whenever they come.

My life has known many trials and sorrows, from childhood to adulthood and every stage in between. I have faced and felt betrayal by family and friends alike, suffered the loss of loved ones, a loss of self, mind, and at times faith.

KEEP GOING!

At my lowest points I wanted to give up completely, to go to sleep and never wake again, because at those times, the pain felt like too much to bear for even a second longer. At my highest points however, I felt like I was capable of anything, I was filled with a love so pure and powerful that it could not be suppressed by the strongest storm or dimmed by the darkest night.

When I had no will of my own to go on, the spirit of God still filled my lungs and kept my heart beating, to eventually see the days that would serve to be some of the greatest of my life thus far. If not for a divine will in me to KEEP GOING, I would have easily forfeited the highlights of my life, only ever knowing the fleeting pain of the lows.

Hindsight is 20/20, and knowing what I know now, just the idea that I would have given up the most precious, most valuable, and cherished moments of my life because of temporary pain and strife is unthinkable at best, and unbearable at worst. This is why it is important to pause in your pain, press into the root of it, and pray your way through it.

KEEP GOING!

Oftentimes we are so overwhelmed and consumed in our most trying moments that we are like a swimmer caught in an undertow, frantically trying to claw, splash, and swim our way onto the shore. However, in the chaos, when the water is bearing down; when you are beneath the surface being twisted and turned in every direction, you need to slow down enough to be able to determine up from down and forward from back. If you don't, you risk losing the breath in your lungs, swimming deeper into the water mistaking down from up, and you risk giving up the last of your strength and stamina swimming further out away from the shore instead of heading into its safety.

"The confusion, and emotion of the situation is what leads to greater peril, not the situation itself." -Alicia Hernandez

By taking the initial step of pausing to gather your bearing and assess what is happening, not through emotion but through facing reality, you begin to allow your mind to make sense of what is happening. What once was a blur of emotion, disjointed, and distorted in your mind, can now be pieced

KEEP GOING!

together for what it really is. Maybe it is a sudden loss, a crisis of identity, or a betrayal. Pausing to make sense and paint a clear picture of whatever has transpired, is the first step in seeing it clearly, and developing a plan of action to overcome, even in situations that will take more time.

I faced a great deal of struggle and uncertainty when my dad was sick. Back in 2011, he was suffering through what, at the time, was an unknown health crisis. I was 21, in college, pregnant with my first child, and my dad landed in the hospital and had to have emergency surgery to prep him for dialysis because his kidneys were failing.

This, mind you was not my first experience with my father falling seriously ill. Several years prior, when I was 15, he went on a trip with some friends and fell ill. So ill, that we had to drive from California to Arizona to pick him up and bring him home. A few days later, while being seen by the doctor, he was rushed in an ambulance to the hospital and treated for a serious case of double pneumonia. I will never forget hearing the doctor say if we had waited, even one more day, to bring him in, he wouldn't have made it.

KEEP GOING!

That experience sat with me for a long time and caused me to fall into a depression that I had to dig my way out of. I wasn't ready to lose my dad, and just the thought that I had been so close to doing so, was more than I knew how to handle.

Sitting there at 21, with a new unknown, and a looming uncertainty as to whether my dad would pull through this new trial or not, left me once again struggling to cope and struggling to make sense of it all. I had to decide what I was going to do for my own health and sanity, and for the health of my unborn baby. I paused, evaluated the situation, and determined that though there may be a lot of unknowns, it was essential that I fight through the emotions that I was feeling, gather myself, and prepare a plan of attack.

Part of the plan for me, at this particular time, was to take a break from school and focus on being there for my family and helping in whatever way I could, and that is exactly what I did. Determining what your plan is going to be, and what your next step is going to look like, does not mean that it will be without sacrifice, or loss, or even without pain, but

KEEP GOING!

it means that you are going to make a thoughtful decision about how to deal with your hard.

When life hits with the unexpected, there is no way out. You can't hit rewind, you cannot go back in time and change the reality of what you are facing, but you can determine how you will face it, and that is what makes all the difference in the world because when you fail to plan a way out when adversity hits, and instead allow the pain and discomfort to overwhelm you, you quickly become overcome *by* that grief instead of learning to overcome your grief.

Leaving school was a small sacrifice to make sure that I could navigate the remainder of my pregnancy, even with all the stress and emotion that was piling on, given everything happening at the time. It allowed me to evaluate what mattered most, and pour all the energy I had into creating the best outcome I could, and also allowed me to make the most out of the situation at hand, as unfortunate as it was.

This is where I was able to press into the root of my pain. Giving myself a moment to first evaluate, and take those initial steps, allowed me to clear both my schedule and my

KEEP GOING!

mind, just enough, to begin to dig deeper and understand where so much of my pain and discomfort was coming from.

Oftentimes, not always, but oftentimes the real root of the pain, is not the occurrence itself but something else. A lot of times the root is not something that is left exposed and easily seen, it is something buried beneath the surface that takes time and diligence to realize and fully discover. This doesn't mean that the challenge itself isn't painful, it simply means that there is something much deeper that is causing the deepest discomfort or is causing your discomfort to be exacerbated and inflamed to such a degree that it can be unbearable.

I was overcome with worry and fear because my dad was sick, and I didn't know what the future held, but beneath that most basic pain was much more that was causing it. I felt vulnerable again, like a child. I was right back in high school remembering when another doctor had informed us my dad had been hours, or a day at most, away from dying. I remembered how nonchalantly he discussed his illness with friends and family over the phone, once he was out of the

KEEP GOING!

hospital, and how angry it made me because of how scared I had been, and how scared I had still felt.

Beneath that, was another layer still, I thought back to when I was 13 and my great-grandma had passed away. She was such an important person to me, and I oftentimes still felt the pain of her loss as though it had just happened. I was still, years later processing the ways that her death had affected me, and I was not ready to lose another key figure in my life again so soon.

Even still, below that was the pain at the idea of losing my dad, and him never meeting my baby that would be born in just a few short months. There was pain at the idea of him never meeting any of his grandkids because she would be the first, and one day my brother would have kids of his own too and it wasn't fair that none of them would ever know their grandpa.

Much of my pain was rooted in the "what if's" and the pain of memories and events past, and yes there was also pain in the here and now, but these other fears and experiences were amplifying it to a much greater degree, and it was

KEEP GOING!

holding me hostage. It was at times crippling me, and leaving me unable to function, unable to do anything other than cry, worry, and then cry some more.

Pressing in and asking myself "what is really going on here?" allowed me to see the pieces of the puzzle that I had been missing and allowed me to better understand the full picture so that I could process it, in its entirety. Now that I could see it, I could face it and begin to deal with it, allowing myself to overcome it, whatever the end result might be.

I had done all I could do on my own and what I now needed most was peace and reassurance that I was unable to give myself. In fact, no one around me could provide the peace that I needed and so desperately craved. It was time to pray. I needed to lay everything out on the table and ask God for His help and reassurance, because on my own, I could only get so far.

I knew that without His help, no matter how rationally I tried to think things through, no matter how much I tried to plan for one outcome or another, I would ultimately lose my

KEEP GOING!

grip and my sanity, falling back into my own fears, doubts, and pain.

I remember praying as soon as my dad ended up in the hospital, of course, but that prayer was different from this one. That prayer was frantic and desperate, and though I know God hears all prayers, even the ones we keep in our hearts when we don't have the words to speak, I knew I needed to articulate what I now needed, and so I prayed.

"God, give me peace at this moment, in this situation. Give me the strength and resolve that I need to navigate what is happening and give me the wisdom and guidance I need to get through it. I cannot do this alone. Remove the troubles and fears of my heart and grant me the peace only you can give. Comfort me in my weakness and give me the reassurance, that no matter what happens we will all be okay."

There wasn't an overnight shift of circumstances, but there was a new sense of peace inside of me. There wasn't a lack of emotion, or at times, even feelings of doubt, but there was a definite covering in the peace that surpasses understanding. There was still a long road ahead but I was

KEEP GOING!

better able to pause, press in, and pray, whenever I needed to and I would definitely need to.

I delivered a healthy baby girl in January of 2012, and my dad would just be starting his journey on dialysis which was long and hard. Statistically, the odds were not good, and his best hope would be a transplant but there was a long road before that would even be an option.

It was on this road that they discovered my dad had cancer on one of his kidneys, something that would not have otherwise been discovered, had it not been for the rigorous testing they do to approve someone to even be on the transplant list. This led to a partial nephrectomy to remove the cancer, which was found early enough that he never even needed chemo. However, it also required he be two years cancer free before being eligible for the list, with credit for time served. I watched my dad lose his strength, his energy, and his appetite, and spend almost 5 years mostly bedridden.

I had to constantly follow these steps: Pause, Press in, and Pray. Life continued to happen all around me. Other setbacks, other struggles, heartbreaks, betrayals, and losses

KEEP GOING!

while one of my life's most challenging trials continued to play in the background. Had I not determined early on that I was going to KEEP GOING no matter what, I would not have made it through.

I now had my baby girl, and she gave me a level of focus and strength to continue fighting that I never would have had otherwise. She was truly heaven-sent, despite the circumstances during her arrival, she was critical to getting through countless days and nights where fear would creep in and threaten to get the best of me. She also gave my dad the will to KEEP GOING.

Prior to her birth, he seemed resolved to go with the flow and not put up much of a fight, but she gave him something to fight for. This tiny human bonded with him on the same level I had bonded with my great-grandmother, and she gave his heart the will to keep beating, as tired as his body might be.

Over and over through the years, after losing another great matriarch in our family, losing a very close friend tragically and unexpectedly, facing new health scares and

KEEP GOING!

illness, and so much more it has become imperative for me to start off every challenge in this same way. There is no magic pill or secret that can steer us clear of adversity and pain, there are only things we can do to help remedy situations when they arise and help us get through what feels like impossible circumstances.

It is important to remember that the pain we feel, is not the end, because there is so much more to life than loss, and some things must end for others to begin. It is not always easy, but it is always possible to overcome those moments that threaten to consume us. It can't be done alone but thankfully the only one we need on our side is on our side; all we have to do is ask for His help.

When troubles arise and things get hard, I remind myself who the captain of the ship is, and I trust Him to navigate me through the deepest, darkest waters, through even the worst storms. I pause and evaluate the situation, press in and look for the root of my discomfort, and pray for peace, wisdom, comfort, and whatever else I need to see me through.

KEEP GOING!

I do these things as often as I need to do them, and without fail, each and every time, they give me the strength to KEEP GOING.

KEEP GOING!

"Churched Out"

Author: C.R. Lundy

My grandmother attended The Salvation Army Corps. My mother was a staunch Catholic and attended St. Joseph's early Mass each Sunday before work. As for me, I went where and when I was told as most Bahamian children were. As with the majority of Bahamians, going to church was never an option but a commandment basically, "Thou shalt go to church or feel the wrath of thy parents".

Being "churched" is a serious part of Bahamian upbringing whether Baptist, Presbyterian, Anglican Pentecostal or any other denomination. Church is ingrained from childhood into adulting whether appreciated or agreed upon, but to church you must go. It is expected and

KEEP GOING!

understood that church attendance is indubitably a part of a Bahamian's makeup.

I have no legitimate argument for or against this practice, only a personal epiphany of recognizing that I am 'churched out.' Going to church was and is not an issue for me. I've always looked forward to Sunday's go-to meeting time. It was not a task at least not the livelier services; I love the hand clapping, tambourine playing, informative messages, made-up faces and people 'catchin' the spirit.

In my adult years, I gravitated to the Salvation Army and enrolled there as a soldier (member), and served in various capacities. Eventually, I got married there, dedicated our children there, and grew them up in the church there.

Let me say "churched" is generally understood to be the practice of attending Sunday or Sabbath service at the edifice of choice or familiarity. "Churched" is being present at weekly meetings whether Bible Study, Prayer Meeting, Youth Fellowship, choir practice, Sunday/Sabbath School, Women's or Men's Ministry at a spiritual establishment to fit in and be considered acceptable and respectable. Once

KEEP GOING!

'churched' it is expected to be carried through in clothing worn, speaking 'churchese' (my word) and the company that you keep.

I identify 'churched out' to feeling overly dictated to and mandated by church leadership, and some membership, to rules, regulations and orders that are exaggerated and have nothing to do with The Almighty's commandments, principles and precepts. You may be familiar with the comments and conversations; "Well, why wasn't you at the women's retreat, recital or whatever" or "Nah, Sister Lundy you been missing prayer meeting often" or my all-time pain "Why you wasn't ta church on Sunday".

Then there's the ones who judgmentally inquire about your children, "Nicki, ain't coming to youth night eh?", "What happen Dee wasn't in the Thanksgiving program?" or "Why your children don't come to Sunday school?". Personally, I believe and have tried to practice 'train up a child in the way he/she should go" adage but not to the detriment of their own spiritual development. If you don't know even children get church burnout so it can be important to give them some voice

KEEP GOING!

and space. So I always tried to keep our children involved but not engulfed in church activities.

Mind you, some persons are genuinely concerned and are interested in you being a part of the Christian community. However, there are too many who are practicing their Pharisee importance and I no longer have a quarter to give. I have received, without invitation, an abundance of unwarranted and unnecessary direction from uninformed churched members who know not of what they speak. I continued to attend mostly due to my obligation as a long-standing member and knowing it was expected of me. I participated in the services to help out as part of the church's membership whether I was being spiritually fueled and fulfilled or not.

In a way, I thank the heavens for the global pandemic in 2020 as it gave me a breather. It was impossible because of the lockdowns to attend physical services and it granted me the chance to reflect, release, and refuel. There was no reason to get dressed, genuflect, 'tourist smile', ingratiate oneself or tolerate unwanted church advice. And so, I came to recognize that I am church tired, church exhausted, and drained from the

KEEP GOING!

expectation of church folk but I didn't know how was I to admit and resolve this and still keep my church card.

Thankfully, Holy Spirit prompted me to the knowledge that on my deepest level I am not accountable to church people but to The Establisher of the church.

In my obedience to my convictions, I began to bow out gracefully from responsibilities and attendance. Of course, peoples' understanding and acceptance were not positive; although I knew their thoughts were 'Sister Lundy must be going somewhere else' as my husband attends another church. I have had to respectfully decline comment and hold my peace, since I had not been convicted to give an explanation (I guess I awaited this platform).

Divine Confirmation

I visited my 95-year-old grandmother in December 2021 and something she said spun my head and gave me pause. We were talking about how she managed while living alone during the lockdowns without visitors, and as she is extremely hard of hearing, she had limited phone

KEEP GOING!

conversations. She said to me "You know Chris, I've come to realize God knows exactly where I am at all times and He and I worship together straight through." Well lick me with a stick, here I was thinking I couldn't stop 'churching' because God may not always show up where I am if I'm not with other like-minded individuals, and my grandmother, as she usually does, spoke into my spirit godly wisdom.

One other thing that happened, on January 1, 2022, was the loss of my beloved uncle. This hit hard (even as I write I'm tearing up) as he was my sounding board and confidante. He lived abroad, so whenever we got on the phone, we would discuss just about everything without judging or correcting or thinking badly about the other; we would enjoy engaging and wonderful conversations just respecting each other's lives and veracities. He was funny, blunt, and generous, always looking forward to his visits back home to The Bahamas.

I remember on his last trip home he said to me "You know niece that pastor ya'll have ain't making no sense you might as well preach to yourself." After his demise and

KEEP GOING!

through my grieving this recollection came back to me and I recognized I was accepting mediocrity in my spiritual growth. I was staying where I was because I was comfortable and becoming lazy in my experience. However, I knew this is not what I am meant to experience in my spiritual journey. I am to be enthused, involved, empowered, and impassioned in and with my Divine connection.

So, what was my remedy to my churched-outness...I've discontinued membership to one specific denomination or church. I've given up my pew and, in my case my uniform and insignia. I made a decisive choice to distance myself from the involvement of any single entity and I am worshiping as influenced by my spiritual connection. In doing so, these are the factors that I take into account as I maintain and seek to deepen this connection, which I share with you as they may assist you with doing the same:

BREATHE. Inhale. Exhale. Feel and listen to your breathing. Concentrate on it. Shallow breaths. Deep breaths. God breaths. Our Creator's first act upon forming man from the dust was to breathe into His unique creation as reflected in

KEEP GOING!

Genesis 2:7, *"Then the LORD God formed a man from the dust of the ground and breathed into his nostrils the breath of life, and the man became a living being"*. This is the first step to keep going; plainly and simply by breathing and appreciating existence as a part of The Creator's plan for and in the universe.

ACCEPT WHO I AM. Acknowledge that I am a living temple of The Most High God. I exist as a place for the Holy Spirit to abide in because of my divine relationship. Value my role as 'the church' even if I am not in a physical building. When Jesus left the earth He sent The Comforter Who resides within me and churches me. He convicts, corrects, and instructs in day-to-day living as I permit Him. I am *the created* for **The Creator**. I am here for His pleasure to church wherever I am and whenever I please. I am not limited or bound by space or a place only by choice. I am capable of churching without having to enter a built structure because I am made to do so.

OBEDIENCE. The refrain "to not forsake or forget the gathering of believers" is quoted to endear persons to

KEEP GOING!

return to the church building. It is a reminder to which I hold. I can and will attend more than one place of worship. I can and will worship with fellow believers sometimes on a Saturday or sometimes on a Sunday. I will be obedient to the leading of the Holy Spirit and interact, share, inspire, and uplift others who believe as I do but it will not be from obligation but because I am prompted by Holy Spirit to do so at an appointed time and worship space.

BELIEVE. I am convinced that God is God. I not only believe in God; I believe God. I believe in the Trinity. I believe that Jesus is the Son of God who died and rose and is alive. I believe that the Holy Spirit indwells within believers and enables us to fully realize our Christian experience. Therefore, I steadfastly believe that a concrete building does not constrain the manifestation of The Almighty. Worshiping without entering an edifice is possible and acceptable. My spiritual relationship is not stronger or lesser once I step in or out of a structure. I know, that I know, *that I know* I am a part of God's divine family, and being unchurched does not detract from that FACT.

KEEP GOING!

Now as you're reading this you may not be unchurched but frustrated, distant, troubled, discouraged, or questioning your present spiritual stance. You haven't given clear thought, voice, or action to doing anything about your feelings because you truly don't know what should or can be done.

Here are a few truths to ponder and remember:

- Your Father God loves you. This is a fact and nothing nor anyone changes this fact. He loves you no more today than yesterday and will love you no less tomorrow. He loves you wherever you are: whether you're in a pew, on the beach, in the park, or in bed. Wherever you are, GOD loves you!
- Romans 12:2 states *"Do not conform any longer to the pattern of this world, but be transformed by the renewing of your mind."* Therefore, change your thought patterns. Speak to yourself and post notes reminding you that you are chosen and called by Christ and His Name, and not by a church.

KEEP GOING!

- Remain open to the Holy Spirit and His prompting daily to walk in integrity and honour Him.
- Never feel any less spiritually attached to The Divine because you are not sitting in church as you are already of a royal priesthood if you have accepted His invitation to be in a relationship with Him.
- Romans 11:36 *"For everything comes from Him and exists by His power and is intended for His glory."* You are meant for God. He created you and you exist for Him……..not for the women's ministry, fundraising committee, or deacon board. You belong to Him first and foremost.
- Involve God in everything you do. He should always be your CENTER. Your life should not be separated into sacred and secular. All of what you do and who you are at all times should represent Him. Acts 17:28 tells us *"For in Him we live and move and have our being. As some of your own poets have said, 'We are His offspring.'"*
- Live your life with and for God as directed in Colossians 3:17 *"And whatever you do, in word or*

KEEP GOING!

deed, do everything in the name of the Lord Jesus, giving thanks to God The Father through Him." Be churched in God and give little heed to the opinions and feedback of others. You are accountable to Him.

Although churched out I am determined to maintain my spiritual relationship with The Creator. I will move through this season and make it to the next. Ecclesiastes 3 speaks of times and seasons, and the only time or season that is not stated is a time to quit or give up. As a matter of fact, the scriptures clearly state in Galatians 6:9 *"Let us not grow weary or become discouraged in doing good, for at the proper time we will reap, if we do not give in."* Therefore, even though we may be in a season of spiritual drought we are to keep going, keep pushing, keep churching if not in an edifice then wherever and in whatever state The Almighty meets us.

Throughout scripture, we read of mighty spiritual men and women, and speak of people of great faith but guess what? When these individuals were in those seasons they did not know or recognize their spiritual might or greatness. They themselves were churched out in their experiences with doubt,

KEEP GOING!

despair, and sometimes defeat. Men like David, Elijah, and Moses had to be encouraged and reassured by the Spirit of God to keep going. Subsequently, their lives and their stories empower us on our spiritual sojourns. It is, therefore, my hope that my experience will do the same for others.

I may be churched out but I will keep going because I have Christ within. I have the reassurance of the songwriter's pen that wrote "He lives, He lives, Christ Jesus lives today; He walks with me and talks with me along life's narrow way". I am unchurched but I am never disconnected.

In some endings there are new beginnings as God can bury the old and makes all things new as in 2 Corinthians 5:17 *"Therefore if anyone be in Christ, that person is a new creature: old things are passed away; behold, all things are become new."*

I know He is renewing and refreshing me for even more. I've come to appreciate that no one is responsible to work out my salvation but me, and since I desire a deeper spiritual relationship it requires my own input and attention.

KEEP GOING!

In having re-evaluated my life and how I allow circumstances and people to affect my time; my mindset; my space; knowing I have lived more years than I may have remaining it is vital that I spend the remainder of my time wisely and honestly.

I am engaging daily in devoting time and opportunity to interactions with Him. My assurance is He is with me and, like John 15:4 commands *"Remain in Me, as I also remain in you. No branch can bear fruit by itself; it must remain in the vine. Neither can you bear fruit unless you remain in Me,"* I will be fruitful, cleaving and not leaving His covering.

Even though I may not attend church regularly I am never out of God's Purpose or Presence. My Father is there for me, and with Him, I will *Keep Going*.

KEEP GOING!

"Unwavering Faith"

Author: Denise D. Beneby

I looked out at the clouds as the American Airline jet continued its ascent. As I sat in my window seat, I remembered how as children, my friends and I used to look at the clouds and try to distinguish what shapes they resembled. But at that moment sitting on the plane, for some reason, the clouds look shapeless. Maybe, it was just that my mind was blank and had a lot on it at the same time. You see, that plane ride was like no ordinary plane ride. That one was different.

A week earlier I had gotten the news that my oldest sister Daphne, who had been fighting breast cancer, had but a few more days to live. The report I got was that there was nothing else the doctors could do for her; a nurse had recommended that she get her affairs in order. Oh no!! Not

KEEP GOING!

Daffy (our pet name for her). I remember her being a pillar of strength for my aunt Bessie and my mother when they both had their breast cancer diagnosis. My aunt died; in fact, she was my mother's second sister to die from cancer and by the time we found out about Daphne's cancer my mother would have already buried her three sisters from cancer. Thankfully, my mother's breast cancer was caught in time.

As my mother's second daughter, I felt that it was my duty to be my sister's source of encouragement. The only problem with that was that I was thousands of miles away in Arkansas having just completed my MBA through Harding University. I was currently working on campus on my Optional Practical Training (OPT), which allowed international students to work in their field of study for a year to get vocational experience. I was paid about $8 to $10 an hour.

My husband was also a student at Harding University, and our sons were in elementary and high schools. So, finding the funds to go and see my sister would require some financial juggling on our part. Knowing that my other siblings would

KEEP GOING!

be there for Daffy, at this time, brought me some comfort. However, I knew that I wanted to be there and I prayed to God that I would get to see my sister for one last time. I shared my situation with my colleague Teresa McCleod. Being a breast cancer survivor herself, she saw the urgency of my situation and told me to leave it to her. Two days later I had my ticket in my hand to the Bahamas. The Lord provided! To this day I have no idea who contributed to my ticket, but I will forever be grateful to them.

On that plane as I was heading home, looking at the awesomeness of God in the beauty of the clouds, I could not help but call out to Him, "Lord please let her be alive when I get there, and I will serve you for the rest of my life." I know it's silly how we feel that we can make a deal with God: "Lord if you do this, then I will do that…." I know, as a Christian, I ought to serve God and be faithful to Him for the rest of my life, but in my emotional state, I thought I had something to bargain for with God.

When Daphne saw me, she was "wide-eyed" and surprised. She said, "Girl, what are you doing here?" and then,

KEEP GOING!

"Everybody coming hey?" I know that I was a welcomed help for my mother because I took over day-to-day dealings with my sister. I made green drinks for her, as I read that they are good for cancer patients. I also took her to get her bandages changed because her breast started to leak, as she had not had surgery to remove her breast.

I recall walking through the hospital and the stares from other patients, as her breast was the size of a basketball and she easily lost her balance as she fell once or twice, but my sister walked with her head held high and for those who did not notice her at first, they noticed her afterward because she made a point of saying, "Good morning," as she kept stepping.

When her bandages were changed, people left the area because the stench was so overwhelming. It was through that experience that my appreciation grew for nurses. They treated her with so much respect and cleaned her breast up before bandaging it; to do it all over again in the next two days.

Although I thought it would have been longer, I am grateful that the Lord allowed me to spend ten days with Daffy

KEEP GOING!

before He took her "home" on April 7th, 2012. I went with her in the ambulance because she was having difficulty breathing. Earlier in the day she had seen something crawling on the walls and she had family members up and down, checking under the bed to see if it had crawled there. It dawned on me that my friend's husband "saw" the same thing before he died.

Reality hit me like a ton of bricks. My sister was getting ready to depart. She had also stopped talking. I thought about all the unfulfilled plans that my sister had, the dreams for her two children, and the fact that she would not see her granddaughter grow up, or any other grandchildren for that matter. How would she be remembered?

Memories of my sister flooded my thoughts. I remembered how she liked salt on everything, especially watermelon. She liked hot sausage and pickles. She was such a fancy dresser, and I could not wait to get her hand-me-downs. She would sometimes lend me her clothes and she was very kind. When my younger sisters and I were going through changes in our bodies it was she who explained what was happening.

KEEP GOING!

We were so grateful that she knew how to braid and fix our hair because our grandmother used to fix our hair with those "hog plaits" that were so big that they never laid flat but stuck out. I remember her getting disciplined by my grandmother because she let one of her friends redo her hair after the boys teased her about her "hog plaits."

I remembered she decided to give up on being a hairdresser despite the fact that she went to Willisy's and studied Cosmetology, and she was really good at it; I think she got discouraged because people used to come to her to get their hair styled and they did not want to pay. I encouraged her to go to the Industrial Training College, which is now the Bahamas Technical and Vocational Institute (BTVI). She told me that when she was in school, she did not want to be in school, and now that she is out of school, she's not going back to school. But she encouraged the rest of us in our higher learning aspirations, and also encouraged Rhondia and D'Ron, her children, to excel. She was so proud of us and she never forgot to let us know it. She always ended her calls with, "love you girl."

KEEP GOING!

Ongoing Challenges

My mother's cancer came back but this time in the ovary. This became more obvious because her stomach was bloated and did not go down but continued to grow. I read somewhere that by the time bloating and pain occur from ovarian cancer it is too late. Mommy said that she wished they had told her to take out her reproductive organs when she had surgery for her breast.

By this time, she was a ten-year breast cancer survivor. If I had known then that my mother was going to follow my sister two years and ten months later, I would have started her on green drinks and live foods sooner. I would have told her that I loved her a little more and asked her to forgive me for being the stubborn child that I was growing up.

They gave my mother three months to live. But at that time, I saw a fighting spirit in her that was not easily defeated. She said, "God did not bring me this far to leave me now!" and "Why worry when you can pray!" Yes, she had beaten cancer once before and she was determined to do it again. She

KEEP GOING!

got radiation to shrink the cancer and she was getting chemotherapy, as well.

I remember when the doctor told us that the therapy was not working and we both cried and hugged each other. I told her that she was going to be all right and she said, "Oh yes, by the grace of God." She spoke to my stepsister, Bertha, later on, and said, "The doctor said ain't nothing change, but in spite of the situation, you got to give God thanks for everything." Mommy was often in a lot of pain because the fluid was not draining, but she was still able to say, "Give thanks to Almighty God for what you got!"

Mommy got comfort from me reading the Psalms to her. Her favorite ones were Psalms 23, 35, 46, and 121. She knew Psalms 121 by heart and often recited it. These scriptures still bring me comfort today. The doctors gave her two to three months to live, and she lasted six months. I will forever be thankful for the time I was able to spend with my mother and make even more memories with her.

Some people are not given the opportunity to spend time with their loved ones because death sometimes comes

KEEP GOING!

suddenly. I thought I was going to have more time with Daffy, but I did not and missed out on the opportunity to record a message for her children. I learned from that experience and got mommy to do a video recording for each of her children and grandchildren. She also did it for some of her nieces, nephews, and friends.

The one that got my uncle so emotionally "worked up" was the one we recorded for the church and was played at her funeral. In the recording, she thanked everyone for everything that they did for her and she encouraged them to keep praying. Prayer and her strong belief in her God led my mother to keep going.

Someone once told me that Bahamians should not have any stress because living in the Bahamas we are surrounded by sun, sand, and sea. In other words, we can relax at the beach every day. If only it were that easy. Most of the time our minds would not allow us to relax because we are so busy cramming it full of the problems that we are faced with on a daily basis: sick parent, sick spouse, childrens school fees, mortgage or rent due and you have no idea where the

KEEP GOING!

money is going to come from to pay either, the list seems endless.

I try to see what lessons I can learn from different situations in my life. You may be feeling overwhelmed as you read this chapter, because of what you may be going through. You may feel like there is no way out or that everyone has turned their back on you. You may be missing your confidant, like a mother or sister, who you always turned to for help or a listening ear. You may feel like you are unable to keep going. I want to share with you some lessons that I learned from dealing with my sister and mother that were a great help to me, and I know will help you cope, as you deal with your difficult situations that may involve long-term illness or even death.

First of all, develop a deep relationship with your God. This relationship comes through obedience to God's word. Many times, people only remember God when they go through a tragedy. Sadly, when God is supposed to be our first thought, He ends up being an afterthought instead.

KEEP GOING!

Secondly, pray. This can be for yourself or others. I remember when my mother became a Christian, she wanted to be useful and was asked by one of the church's deacons to call those who were shut in and encourage them. My mother not only called them, but she also prayed with them. This eventually evolved into her very own prayer ministry.

A few months after my mother's funeral one of the sisters at church told me that she missed my mother praying for her on Wednesdays. Upon further inquiry, she told me that when her phone rang at seven in the morning, on Wednesdays, she knew that that was Sister Belle calling her to pray with her. I found my mother's black book. In this book she kept the numbers and times that she would call each person.

During the lockdown, due to the COVID - 19 pandemic, I had some spare time, as I am sure all of us did. I decided to call some people up to encourage them, and as a result, I was encouraged as I would end each call with a prayer. When you take time to pray for others, you will forget all about your own problems or they will seem minute. I can now understand the joy that my mother experienced with each

KEEP GOING!

call she made and the pleasure each recipient got from her calls.

Thirdly, never give up. As I mentioned earlier, my sister fell once or twice because of the weight of her breast, but she got back up each time. My mother battled cancer twice and she kept fighting to the very end. I too have had my share of health problems, and I made up my mind that I will not give in or give up.

Fourthly, keep trusting God. When my sister was given just a few more days to live, I did not know how I was going to make it home to be able to see her, but I believed that the Lord was going to work it out and He did. This trust was also evident in my own health concerns.

I remember that I kept going to the doctor and I did test after test and of course, the first thing that came to my mind was cancer. After all, I had a family history of it; my mother, her three sisters, my sister, and my father and his two sisters had all succumbed to this tragic disease. However, I knew that God was going to work it out. Yes, I also had a part to play! I took the BRCA gene test which came back negative,

KEEP GOING!

changed my diet, and started exercising. I started thinking positive thoughts and knew that I had to think about prevention rather than cure.

Whenever I go through aches and pains in my body, I reflect on Job 1:8 where the Lord asks Satan if he has considered His servant Job. I would substitute Job's name with my name and know that just as Job went through his problems and was able to overcome them because he trusted God, I too will overcome anything that I face.

Next, make new memories. I knew that our mother was going to leave us soon. I also knew that when she did, we were no longer going to hear her voice, which is why I made a recording for each of her children giving them words of encouragement. Some of my siblings say that they were not brave enough to listen to the recording but had comfort in knowing that it was there whenever they wanted to listen.

While I grieved for my mother it was easier because I knew that she was a Christian first and foremost, so I had that reassurance that we were going to see each other again. Easier still because I spent time with her. I took her for rides to the

KEEP GOING!

beach, spent time talking about her childhood, and invited some of her childhood friends over to visit with her and they reminisced even more about their childhood. My mother was still above ground and while she spent time in her bedroom, she did not need to spend her remaining days only staring at the four walls.

You may not have been given the time to spend with your loved one before they died but you still have the memories of them that you carry with you every day. Put pen to paper and write down some of those memories and share them, and you can even have a day of reflection on the person's birthday or the anniversary of their death.

Lastly, some of you may be grieving for someone who is still alive and would have hurt you deeply by their absence as in the case of a divorce or an incident where your best friend or a family member has stopped speaking to you. Make peace first of all by forgiving the person who may have offended you or whom you may have offended.

In his book "I Forgive, An Inner Lane Towards Forgiveness", my husband Kevin has chapters entitled 'It

KEEP GOING!

Hurts' and 'The Option of Forgiving'. In those chapters, it is clearly pointed out that unforgiveness can negatively impact our lives from a physiological, psychological, functional, and relational perspective. He noted that "while the yoke of unforgiveness can be borne, because of its oppressive and burdensome qualities for those who carry it, it really becomes a means of self-sabotage. Individuals can do great injury to themselves if they allow the emotion of unforgiveness to take root and fester in their lives." It is definitely in our best interest to forgive others and still move on or we would only hurt and damage ourselves.

I have a friend who lost her mother a few years ago. She told me that she prayed and prayed to God to spare her mother's life, but He still allowed her to die. Sadly, she turned her back on God. After my mother's funeral, my youngest son, who was nine years old at the time, hugged me and told me something that he had once mentioned when I lost a friend a few years prior. He said, "Mommy don't be sad that grammy is gone but be glad that she was here." He was trying to encourage me, and he did just that, because I was able to reflect on the timeless wisdom of his words. I was glad that

KEEP GOING!

my mother had been here. Glad that she was able to obey the gospel of Christ. Glad that she did not die when I was a young girl growing up and needed her the most, glad she met her grands and great-grands. Why are you glad that your loved ones were here? Think about it. It helps. It heals.

It is my hope that you have gleaned something from this chapter that would have encouraged and strengthened your faith in God or towards God. Regardless of the loss of a loved one, sickness, loss of a job and the list can go on, know that where there is life there is hope, so in all things give thanks.

As a seventeen-year-old new Christian, I learned a scripture verse that has never disappointed me, even now at fifty, one that I have taught to my sons as they coped with their schoolwork or whatever situation they were faced with, it comes from Philippians 4:13 *"I can do all things through Christ who strengthens me."* With the confidence this scripture provides, one can persevere through life's challenges.

Summary

KEEP GOING!

KEEP GOING!

Summary

Aisha Wonderfull

Here we are....at the end of this book. But just as this book is no ordinary book, this is no ordinary ending. This is an ending that has been Purposefully ordained, appointed and anointed to be *a new beginning for you*. A new beginning to the next level of your own Divine Purpose, and the specific assignment that you have for the next season of your life.

As you have read through these pages, you have gleaned your own lessons from the stories shared by the 10 co-authors of their decision to Keep Going no matter what challenges they faced.

I now invite you to join us.......because no matter your background or national heritage, we all share a common heritage in being daughters of The King, who have our own stories of when we were able to dig down deep and Keep

KEEP GOING!

Going; stories that are divinely purposed to be shared with others.

Not only is it my wish for you to apply the wisdom shared in these pages to your own life, but I ask that you intentionally let these stories, let the stories of these incredible authors soak into you and allow them to unlock and unleash within you your own uniqueness, your own message that you have been given to share with the world.

We have come together. Now, it is time.

Time for you to take up your mantle, time for you to move upward.

Time for you to move onward.

So I leave you with the knowledge that you are ready to step fully, confidently, and BOLDLY into all that you are called to be because RIGHT NOW is a new beginning of the next season of your own journey.

Keep Going!

About the Authors

KEEP GOING!

KEEP GOING!

Aisha "Wonderfull"

As the CEO and Founder of Universal Impact Press, Aisha Jackson helps Purposeful men and women courageously complete the call on their lives to share their stories and write an inspirational book.

KEEP GOING!

Based on her own personal experience and the work that she has done with countless other women, Aisha knows firsthand how powerful writing and publishing a book can be, and how becoming an author allows Purposeful men and women to activate the next level of themselves.

Aisha truly believes that "Your Story May Be About You, but It Is Not For You", and that there are people that **only you** can lead through whatever situation they are facing, the people who are in situations they feel stuck in, or are struggling with, and they are praying for a way out. YOUR sheep are waiting to hear your voice!

Aisha also believed that if you choose to say YES to this amazing call on your life, you are saying YES to making the Universal Impact that you were born to make, and in doing so, you will unleash another level of the powerful, fearfully and wonderfully made version of YOURSELF!

This conviction comes from her own personal experience, and who she has become in the process of saying YES to the call on her own life. But what has been even more

KEEP GOING!

rewarding is who she has become in the process and the change in the way that she sees herself.

Though the name on her ID says Aisha Jackson, when she looks in the mirror, she sees a powerful, Divine creation who was fearfully and wonderfully made in God's image and likeness - and THAT is who Aisha shows up in the world to share her message as: **Aisha WONDERFULL!**

For more information about how you can share your story in an inspirational way, visit www.UniversalImpactPress.com. You can also follow Aisha on Meta (FB) and Instagram: @aishawonderfull.

KEEP GOING!

KEEP GOING!

A. Felicity Darville

Felicity Darville is a dynamic speaker and multi-media professional in Nassau, Bahamas. Her public speaking career started as early as childhood and has evolved into radio and

KEEP GOING!

television presenting, motivational speeches, event hosting and dramatic arts.

During her time as a television journalist, Felicity was inspired to make a positive impact on her country by focusing on getting good news in the news. She wanted to provide more opportunities for community events - and the great stories that came with them - to receive national attention.

Today, she has a track record of success in getting community partners featured in national news. Felicity has used her platform in media to advocate for many causes in the community over the years, including: agriculture and fisheries; youth; women; people living with disabilities; health and wellness; and ending violence and poverty.

She was recognized for her work by the Disability Affairs Unit of the Ministry of Social Services & Urban Development, Government of The Bahamas. She received the 'Media Icon of the Year' award in December, 2021 for consistently partnering with a number of non-government and civic organizations. In the same year, she won an advocacy

KEEP GOING!

champion award from The Bahamas National Breastfeeding Association.

Felicity and her husband, Victor Valentino Darville are both enrolled in an aquaculture degree program at the Bahamas Agriculture & Marine Science Institute, to set a new path to sustainability for their children.

Felicity was trained by one of Britain's best therapists, Marisa Peer in 2017. She now utilizes media to create programs that lead to self-empowerment, such as the youth symposium: #Goals: Make Dreams Reality. Her company, True Vision Media, is now changing its mode of operation from a solo freelancer to a community of highly skilled media professionals.

After decades of crafting the stories of others, Felicity is honored to share her own in this anthology, which she sees as a launching pad for a number of books that are already waiting to be birthed from her soul. To connect further with her, email her at felicitydarville@gmail.com, or visit her social media accounts: Instagram: @empressfelicity/ Facebook: Felicity Darville.

KEEP GOING!

KEEP GOING!

Alicia Hernandez

Alicia Hernandez is an international motivational speaker, bestselling author, women's empowerment coach, and professional writing coach, offering a host of writing services to help others bring their dreams of becoming an author to reality.

KEEP GOING!

Based on her own painful experience as a child and a young adult struggling to fit in, she decided to channel her energy into helping other women gain an understanding of what it means to live a life of inner harmony, peace, and joy by learning to embrace and unlock the potential of the very things that set them apart.

Reaching women around the world, Alicia addresses critical issues affecting women's personal and spiritual development. The central theme of her message is to embrace your uniqueness to maximize your individual potential and thrive, this is something that she is passionate about, and is committed to impacting women worldwide with this message.

She is the founder of One Black Sheep LLC, a lifestyle design company and clothing line that supports women of all ages and backgrounds, as they travel the journey to self-fulfillment by embracing their uniqueness.

Alicia is the proud mom of 4 children: Isabella, Sebastian, Matias, and Rosalie and they reside in Arizona. To learn more about her and her work, visit her website

KEEP GOING!

www.ninetynineforone.com or connect with her on Instagram @aliciahernandez_obsllc.

KEEP GOING!

KEEP GOING!

C.R. Lundy

C.R. Lundy is a mentor, encourager, prayer warrior, confidante, and God-enabler who is passionate about encouraging and inspiring others to have a personal, intimate relationship with The Almighty.

KEEP GOING!

She has made it her mission to direct, point, and lead individuals into that relationship, and support them through maintaining it.

A lifelong resident of The Bahamas, she and her husband of 33 years are the proud parents of 3 young adults.

For the past 21 years, C.R. has worked with The Securities Commission of the Bahamas, where she currently serves as a Supervisor in the Administration Department.

To keep in touch with her, and learn more about the work that she does to support others in their walk with The Almighty, contact her via email @ lundy68chris@gmail.com.

KEEP GOING!

Denise D. Beneby

Denise was born in the tranquil settlement of Fresh Creek, on the island of Andros, Bahamas. She is the third of seven children, raised by a single mother Veronica Belle. Denise aspires to be like the Proverbs 31 wife to her husband of twenty-eight years Kevin, who is currently the full-time

KEEP GOING!

Minister and an Elder at the church of Christ, Highbury Park, in Nassau, Bahamas. Denise and Kevin have been blessed with three sons, Kenan, Abishai, and Denereus.

Denise is a graduate of Harding University, in Searcy Arkansas, where she obtained an MBA in Management and Ethics; a graduate of Nova Southeastern University and the College of the Bahamas, where she obeyed the gospel as a seventeen-year-old student. It was as a student that she came across her favorite scripture verse, which also became her everyday mantra, especially during difficult times, "I can do all things through Christ who strengthens me" (Philippians 4:13). A former social studies, civics, and history teacher and Bahamas General Certificate of Secondary Education (BGCSE) paper setter and marker, Denise is currently employed as a Chief Training Officer at the Ministry of the Public Service through the Public Service Centre for Human Resources Development (PSCHRD).

Denise is passionate about loving those around her just as Christ has so graciously loved us. She enjoys meeting new people and has never "met a stranger."

KEEP GOING!

She thanks God for her communication skills, which have afforded her the opportunity to speak from "His word" passionately. She has presented at Harding University's Annual Lectureships, Annual Caribbean Lectureships, The Commonwealth of the Bahamas Lectureships, seminars, workshops, and has been the keynote speaker at many Ladies Retreats.

Denise believes that everyone has a story to tell. Her mother had a story to tell but sadly her story died with her because she was never able to "accomplish her dream" of telling her story. Based on what they faced together as a family Denise hopes to someday tell some of "her story" for her.

To connect with Denise or to book her to speak at your next Ladies Retreat she can be contacted via email at benebydenise@gmail.com or on Facebook at Denise Taylor-Bencby.

KEEP GOING!

KEEP GOING!

Ednica Newbold

Ednica Newbold is a speaker, #1 bestselling author, coach, and accounting professional.

Based on her own personal experiences as a child growing up in the Bahamas and feeling first-hand the negative effects of the pressure to present the image of a "perfect" life,

KEEP GOING!

(like so many other people who were raised in small communities experience), she has embraced her calling to work with children and not just empower, but also equip them starting at a young age with the necessary skills to live an authentic life.

Ednica is passionate about encouraging others how to cultivate new mindsets and break repeated negative cycles by teaching the importance of authenticity and vulnerability from a young age. She is on a mission to change the perception and narrative of what it means to be "vulnerable," and show others through her own example that when you embrace and lean into vulnerability, it can beneficial to everyone involved.

She is the founder of Cultivate Your Garden, a children's empowerment company that supports children by instilling core values in them. She is also the co-founder of Soul Circle, a community geared towards motivating, inspiring, and helping others to achieve their goals.

Originally from Freeport, Bahamas, Ednica has been a resident of Calgary, Canada since 2011. In addition to her work with Cultivate Your Garden and Soul Circle, she works

KEEP GOING!

full-time as an accountant specializing in internal controls and has both American and Canadian CPA professional designations.

To learn more about Ednica and the work that she does, you can follow her on the following Instagram accounts: @ednican, and @cyg_cultivate_your_garden.

KEEP GOING!

KEEP GOING!

Kay Charlton Cleare

Residing in Nassau, the capital city of the Bahamas, Kay Charlton Cleare is a wife, mother, and entrepreneur who

KEEP GOING!

is passionate about encouraging, motivating, building, and uplifting women and men to be all that they are called to be.

A certified baker & culinary chef whose expertise is in event planning, catering, and sales, in addition to growing her own businesses (The Hygiene Place and The Food Mansion), Kay is kept busy raising 3 beautiful and incredible children to pursue their Purpose in life and also supporting her husband in his entrepreneurial pursuits (Founder of Aquatic Risk Management, a company that offers CPR training and certification individually and to organizations).

She attributes her success in managing all her personal and professional responsibilities to her belief and commitment to putting all she has in for the best results.

This drive has come from her involvement in global marketing (she has been with ARDYSS Int. for several years), and through her active participation and contribution to "Mother Me", a women's organization in the Bahamas.

KEEP GOING!

Kay has plans to continue encouraging and motivating others through other books and has plans to release a solo-authored book.

KEEP GOING!

KEEP GOING!

Krista Barr-Bastian

Krista Barr-Bastian was born and raised in Nassau Bahamas. She is a separated single mother of four beautiful children: Chloe, Dawson, Kruiz, and Kole. A Certified Public Accountant (CPA) by trade, she has a deep passion for women

KEEP GOING!

and seeing them unlock their innate strength to live authoritatively and *fruitfully* as God has commanded.

Very tenacious, she is no stranger to the strife of life having pushed powerfully through seasons of loss, to birth the visions and plans of heaven. *Woman! Push Powerfully** is the first book she has authored. Krista is also the founder of WPP *Worldwide* and *Events by Krista*.

These platforms produce transformational experiences and studies for women, inclusive of its renowned event series *PUSH & EMERGE,* which empowers women to arise out of difficult life-altering seasons renewed and fruitful! You may connect with her at www.kristainspires.com.

KEEP GOING!

Olivia Munroe Ferguson

Olivia is a mother of five (three biological children and two stepchildren), a wife, and also an entrepreneur. Olivia is a strong, independent, God-fearing, resilient, determined, and family-oriented individual.

KEEP GOING!

She is very passionate about helping others. She feels that her purpose is to assist people, whether it be by her using her time, money, or words of encouragement. She feels so accomplished in purposefully doing so.

Olivia has been fortunate to bounce back from adversity and tough challenges in her life, especially her experience of being a teenage mother. These experiences have also given her a keen understanding of the significance of forgiveness and healing, and she believes in sharing these experiences to help other women and mothers heal and release old hurts and pain they experienced so that they can have better relationships with themselves and their children.

As the author of "Still Thriving After Surviving," a book designed to provide motivation and encouragement for other moms who navigated either teenage motherhood or any other motherhood challenge, Olivia is committed to equipping them with personal leadership skills to not only survive but thrive in their roles as a mother to their children.

Olivia has completed a certificate course in Paralegal and one day hopes to fulfill her childhood career dream of

KEEP GOING!

becoming a lawyer. If you would like to connect further with Olivia, she can be reached on her Facebook or Instagram as Olivia Ferguson.

KEEP GOING!

KEEP GOING!

Tashoy Walters

Tashoy Walters is a certified Abundant Life Coach, motivational speaker, humanitarian, philanthropist, and world changer who values dedication, service, and excellence.

KEEP GOING!

As an Abundant Life Coach, and best-selling author, Tashoy is dedicated to seeing people heal, be free and receive the self-love and Abundant Life that is waiting for them. Using real-world examples, Tashoy sheds light on the issue and shows you that it is possible to live a life free from mental negatives and to have an abundantly free clear mind that will activate the belief of "Yes, I Can" and "Yes, I am".

Tashoy believes anything is possible if you believe. She has also tested this thought process by summiting the highest free-standing mountain in Tanzania, Africa.

Tashoy aims to help 1000 women be healed, healthy, whole, solid, and complete through her coaching program "Girl Walk With Me". With this vision and belief, she will also help 1,000 women in Tanzania Africa receive reusable pads to help them heal and have a prayer answered.

Tashoy is a lover of food, traveling, and seeing people win and be their best selves and she wants you to know that **It's time for you to live an Abundant Life!**

KEEP GOING!

To connect with her, she can be found on FB @ Tashoy Walters and IG @tee2thashoy.

KEEP GOING!

KEEP GOING!

Virginia Somerville

Virginia is a resident of Utah in a small town appropriately nicknamed Dinosaurland and is the author of "What About Mom", a book she published in 2021 to help moms of abused children heal their families through love and faith.

KEEP GOING!

She has a wide range of professional experience, gained through her years of working as a nurse, a substitute teacher, a dairy farm manager, a city transit bus driver, as well as a women and child advocate for the court system. The one common thread running amongst all of the professions she has had is her amazing and incredible warmth and love for people.

Based on her own background and upbringing, Virginia is passionate about spreading the love of Jesus to others, and encouraging them to face unexpected challenges that may come their way by being able to pivot effectively, reposition themselves toward a new future, and persevere toward that new future with faith and of most importantly, love.

Virginia is a mother of 5 and grandmother to 13 and proudly counts 3 great-grandchildren at present. Nothing gives her greater joy than spending time with her family, and sharing family traditions passed down from her own grandmother, such as crocheting, and baking her mothers' famous oatmeal softies (which her grandchildren love just as much as her children did)!

KEEP GOING!

Her other hobbies include writing and painting, and she shares her daily life with her service dog Teddy.

KEEP GOING!

UNIVERSAL IMPACT PRESS

Made in the USA
Columbia, SC
30 March 2023